Praise for
In the Line of Fire

"In my role at Cisco Systems, I am confronted with challenging questions from customers, government leaders, press, and analysts on a daily basis. The techniques used in this book, *In the Line of Fire*, are spot on; providing straightforward ways to be on the offense in all communications situations."

Sue Bostrom, Former SVP Internet Business Solutions Group and Worldwide Government Affairs, Cisco Systems

"In an era where businesspeople and politicians unfortunately have proven their inability to be honest with bad news, I believe this book should be prescribed reading in every business school, and for every management training session. In fact, I hope it is read by a far wider audience than that. It's just what our society needs right now."

Po Bronson, author of the bestselling *What Should I Do With My Life?*

"Jerry Weissman tells the tales of the makings of presidents and kings, the dramas of the dramatic moments of our time, and in each episode he uncovers the simple truths behind what makes great leaders like Ronald Reagan and Colin Powell loved and trusted. Great truths made simple and compelling for any leader to use."

Scott Cook, Founding CEO, Intuit

"Jerry's book is a must-read for any presenter facing tough and challenging questions from their audience. This book provides the fundamental foundation on how to prepare, be agile, and take charge no matter how difficult the question."

Leslie Culbertson, Corporate Vice President Director of Corporate Finance, Intel Corporation

"During one of the most important periods of my career, Jerry used the concepts in *In the Line of Fire* to prepare me and my team for the EarthLink IPO road show. He helped us field tough questions from the toughest possible audience: potential investors, but the same skills are necessary for every audience.

Sky Dayton, Founder EarthLink and Boingo Wireless, CEO SK-EarthLink

"Jerry Weissman helped prepare my management team for our recent IPO. I sat in on some of the sessions and was most impressed with Jerry's innovative ways of teaching and optimizing effective executive communication methods. This training, encapsulated well in his new book, *In the Line of Fire*, paid off handsomely during our numerous road show presentations."
Ray Dolby, Founder and Former Chairman, Dolby Laboratories, Inc.

"Whether you're a classroom teacher or the President, this book will help you be an effective communicator. This book is so insightful, reading it feels like cheating. Tough questions no longer test my limits."
Reed Hastings, Founder and CEO, Netflix

"Even the greatest start encounters tough questions. Read Jerry's book before you need it, or you'll be in deep sushi."
Guy Kawasaki, author of the bestselling *Enchantment, Reality Check,* and *The Art of the Start*

"Have you ever been faced with a tough question? Jerry Weissman shows how it's not necessarily what the answer is. It's how you answer that will allow you to prevail and win!"
Tim Koogle, Founding CEO, Yahoo!

"Jerry's technique is both masterful and universal because it finds common ground between audience and speaker, hard questions and direct answers, all with a very simple principle: truth."
Pierre Omidyar, Founder of eBay and Omidyar Network

"I've been asking tough questions for half a century and listening to variously brilliant, boring, evasive or illuminating answers. Jerry Weissman's book will help anyone...anyone...answer even the toughest questions."
Mike Wallace, Senior Correspondent, *60 Minutes,* CBS News

In the Line of Fire

How to Handle
Tough Questions—
When It Counts

In the Line of Fire

How to Handle
Tough Questions—
When It Counts

■ ■ Jerry Weissman ■ ■

Author of
Presenting to Win: The Art of Telling Your Story

An Imprint of Pearson Education
Upper Saddle River, NJ • New York • London • San Francisco • Toronto • Sydney •
Tokyo • Singapore • Hong Kong • Cape Town • Madrid
Paris • Milan • Munich • Amsterdam

Vice President, Publisher: Tim Moore
Associate Publisher and Director of Marketing: Amy Neidlinger
Executive Editor: Jeanne Glasser
Operations Specialist: Jodi Kemper
Cover Designer: Chuti Prasertsith
Managing Editor: Kristy Hart
Senior Project Editor: Lori Lyons
Project Editor: Katie Matejka
Copy Editor: Language Logistics, Christal White
Senior Indexer: Cheryl Lenser
Senior Compositor: Gloria Schurick
Proofreader: Paula Lowell
Art Consultant: Nichole Nears
Manufacturing Buyer: Dan Uhrig

FT Press offers excellent discounts on this book when ordered in quantity for bulk purchases or special sales. For more information, please contact U.S. Corporate and Government Sales, 1-800-382-3419, corpsales@pearsontechgroup.com. For sales outside the U.S., please contact International Sales, 1-317-581-3793, international@pearsontechgroup.com.

Company and product names mentioned herein are the trademarks or registered trademarks of their respective owners.

WIIFY, Point B, Eye Connect, and Topspin are service marks or registered service marks of Power Presentations, Ltd., © 1988–2013.

Courtesies: CNN; ABC News Video Source

© 2004 Gallup Organization. All rights reserved. Reprinted with permission from www.gallup.com.

Printed in the United States of America

First Printing: September 2013

ISBN-10: 0-13-315788-1
ISBN-13: 978-0-13-315788-8

Pearson Education LTD.
Pearson Education Australia PTY, Limited.
Pearson Education Singapore, Pte. Ltd.
Pearson Education Asia, Ltd.
Pearson Education Canada, Ltd.
Pearson Educatión de Mexico, S.A. de C.V.
Pearson Education—Japan
Pearson Education Malaysia, Pte. Ltd.

Library of Congress Control Number: 2013942287

For Lucie…at last.

CONTENTS

▪▪■ Chapter 8: Topspin in Action (Martial Art: Agility)

Missing a Free Kick • The Evolution of George W. Bush • Lloyd Bentsen Topspins • Ronald Reagan Topspins • Barack Obama Topspins

▪▪■ Chapter 9: Preparation (Martial Art: Preparation)

The NAFTA Debate Revisited • Murder Boards • Presidential Elections • Lessons Learned

Case Studies: Al Gore versus Ross Perot; Elena Kagan; John F. Kennedy versus Richard M. Nixon; George W. Bush versus John F. Kerry; Barack Obama versus John McCain; Barack Obama versus Mitt Romney; Cicero

▪▪■ Chapter 10: The Art of War (Martial Art: Self-Control)

The Art of Agility • The Critical Impact of Debates • Lessons Learned

Case Studies: Al Gore debates George W. Bush; Barack Obama debates Mitt Romney

▪▪■ Chapter 11: Lessons *Not* Learned

Reaction Shots • Agreement • Lessons Learned

Case Studies: Al Gore; George W. Bush; Barack Obama; Richard Nixon; Mitt Romney; John F. Kennedy

About the Author

Jerry Weissman, the world's #1 corporate presentations coach, founded and leads Power Presentations, Ltd. in Burlingame, California. His private clients include executives at hundreds of the world's top companies including Intel, IBM, Microsoft, and Cisco Systems.

Weissman coached Cisco's executives before their immensely successful IPO roadshow; afterward, the firm's chairman attributed at least two to three dollars of Cisco's offering price to his work. Since then, he has coached the IPO road shows for nearly 600 companies, helping them raise hundreds of billions of dollars. Among them were Yahoo!, Intuit, Dolby Laboratories, eBay, and most recently Trulia, the real estate search engine company, whose shares jumped more than 40 percent during its first day of trading.

Weissman is author of the global best-selling *Presenting to Win: The Art of Telling Your Story; The Power Presenter: Technique, Style, and Strategy; Presentations in Action: 80 Memorable Presentation Lessons from the Masters;* and *Winning Strategies for Power Presentations* (all published by FT Press/Pearson Education).

INTRODUCTION

Universal Challenges, Universal Solutions

In the eight years since the publication of the first edition of this book, the United States has gone through two contentious presidential elections that put the candidates squarely in the line of fire of tough questions—from their opponents in debates and from the media in interviews. The manner in which those candidates handled those questions had a direct impact on their candidacies and on their ultimate fortunes. Although the political arena has its own rules and idiosyncracies that set it apart from most other walks of life, the manner in which *any* person handles him- or herself in *any* challenging exchange has an impact upon their ultimate fortunes.

And so while this updated second edition, like the original, contains many political examples (because they are more familiar to more people), they have the same dynamics as those many other walks of life: business, finance, government, science, academia, job interviews, and even interpersonal relations. The new examples in this edition represent the same universal challenges as in the original, and so the same universal solutions still apply, demonstrating their staying power.

The universal dynamics of Q&A extend into *all* aspects of *all* presentations, if not *all* communications—a fact supported by the opinions of leading practitioners in other fields of communications. I have studied and collected the advice of experts in literature, cinema, theater, advertising, media, as well as politics, in two other books, *Presentations in Action* and *Winning Strategies for Power Presentations,* and related them to the entire spectrum of presentation skills. Taken together with my three original books, *Presenting to Win,* about the fundamentals of story development and graphics design, *The Power Presenter,* about the fundamentals of delivery skills, and this book about the fundamentals of handling tough questions, they form a thorough methodology to help you or any presenter succeed.

▬▬■ Handling Tough Questions Counts

This comprehensive methodology arose out of my 40 years in the communications trade, which ranged from the control rooms of the CBS Broadcast Center in Manhattan to the conference rooms of Silicon Valley's hottest startups and the boardrooms of some of America's most prestigious corporations. In those rooms, I have heard—and have asked—some very tough questions. As a result, I came to fully understand the potential upside—and downside— impact of how presenters handle challenging exchanges.

That impact was best expressed by Theodore H. White, the noted political historian who chronicled the seminal presidential debates between John F. Kennedy and Richard M. Nixon in his classic book, *The Making of the President 1960.* Mr. White wrote that debates "give the voters of a great democracy a living portrait of two men under stress and let the voters decide, by instinct and emotion, which style and pattern of behavior under stress they preferred in their leader." [I.1]

On one fateful late September evening in 1960, voters decided that they preferred John Kennedy over Richard Nixon as their leader. In that one night the challenger vaulted ahead of the favorite.

Forty-eight years later, another series of late September exchanges produced another political reversal of fortune. At the beginning of that month, Alaska Governor Sarah Palin, having been chosen as the Republican vice presidential nominee, delivered a powerful acceptance speech at the Republican National Convention in St. Paul, Minnesota. That one fiery speech electrified the country and vaulted Arizona Senator John McCain, who had been trailing in the public opinion polls, to a lead over then Illinois Senator Barack Obama. [I.2]

But later that month, Palin was interviewed by *CBS Evening News* anchor Katie Couric. Persistent journalist that she is, Couric pressed Palin on her qualifications to be vice president, particularly her foreign policy credentials. Palin was only able to offer her state's proximity to Russia but nothing more of substance.

The television critic of the *New York Times* reported that the "exchange was so startling it ricocheted across the Internet...it may be hard for Mr. McCain's running mate to recoup. It wasn't her first interview on national television, but in some ways it was the worst." [I.3]

The interview ricocheted into a skit on NBC's *Saturday Night Live*, in which actress Tina Fey, doing an uncannily accurate impersonation of Palin, mocked the remark about the proximity to Russia.

By the end of that month, Barack Obama vaulted back into the lead in the public opinion polls and held it until his victory in November.

Three years later, another September exchange produced another reversal of fortune. A month earlier, when Texas Governor Rick Perry formally announced his candidacy for the Republican presidential nomination, he was late to the party: A large field of candidates had been engaging in a series of televised debates since May of that year. [I.4]

By the time Perry threw his hat into the ring, former Massachusetts Governor Mitt Romney had moved into the lead. But Perry had a rich array of assets. He had won three consecutive gubernatorial races, was the darling of the influential conservative wing of the Republican Party, and had an abundant war chest of campaign finances. Within one month after his announcement, he vaulted to the top of the public opinion polls.

But then on September 22, 2011, he participated in a live televised debate with the other Republican candidates. At one point, following Romney's discussion of how his current health care proposal related to the one he had developed while he was the Massachusetts governor, *Fox News* moderator Chris Wallace—seeking to create conflict—asked Perry to respond:

> PERRY: *I think Americans just don't know sometimes which Mitt Romney they're dealing with. Is it the Mitt Romney that was on the side of against the Second Amendment before he was for the Second Amendment? Was it—was before he was before the social programs, from the standpoint of he was for standing up for Roe v. Wade before he was against Roe v. Wade? He was for Race to the Top, he's for Obamacare, and now he's against it. I mean, we'll wait until tomorrow and—and—and see which Mitt Romney we're really talking to tonight. [I.5]*

The convoluted ramble reverberated throughout the media; the video clip was replayed endlessly on YouTube and by the late night television comics who punctuated it with mocking commentary. Within two weeks, Perry's poll numbers plummeted to almost half of what they had been.

On November 9, he participated in another live television debate in which CNBC moderator Maria Bartiromo asked him what programs he would cut to reduce the deficit. Perry started his answer by saying that he would eliminate three agencies and named Commerce and Education but froze on the third. He struggled for several painful moments to recall, and then gave up, infamously saying, "Ooops!" But by that time, his fate was virtually sealed.

Three months later Perry dropped out of the race. [I.6]

On April 20, 2010, BP's offshore oil drilling platform in the Gulf of Mexico exploded, claiming 11 lives and causing massive environmental damage. The company's CEO, Tony Hayward, whose annual compensation was $4.5 million, when asked what he would tell people in Louisiana, said, "We're sorry for the massive disruption it's caused their lives. There's no one who wants this over more than I do. I would like my life back."

Hayward's "I would like my life back" statement whipsawed throughout the media with the same speed and intensity as did Palin's and Perry's mishandled answers. Within days, Hayward was asked to step down, and four months later, he was fired. [I.7]

Very few people have to deal with a disaster as enormous as an oil spill, and very few people get to run for president of the country, yet few people on the face of this planet get to sail through life without being confronted with tough questions. The purpose of this book and its many real-life examples is to provide you with the skills to handle such questions—and only such questions. If all the questions you are ever asked were to be of the "Where do I sign?" variety, you could spend your time with a good mystery novel instead.

Forewarned is forearmed.

One other forewarning: All the techniques you are about to learn require that you deploy them with absolute truth. The operative word in the preceding paragraph, as well as on the cover of this book, is "handle," meaning how to *manage* tough questions. Although providing an answer is an integral part of that "handling," every answer you give to every question asked of you must be honest and straightforward. If not, all the other techniques will be for naught. With a truthful answer as your foundation, all these techniques will enable you to survive, if not prevail, in the line of fire.

Agility Versus Force

■■■ Challenging Questions

To understand how to handle tough questions, let's begin with the reason people ask such questions. Journalists such as Katie Couric and Chris Wallace (the son of the legendary provocative interrogator Mike Wallace) ask tough questions because, being familiar with the classical art of drama, they know that conflict creates drama. Aristotle 101.

One of the most regularly occurring examples of journalistic baiting is in presidential press conferences. Every U.S. president, regardless of party affiliation, periodically faces the slings and arrows of tough questions from the White House press corps. One such exchange took place on June 23, 2009. In a press briefing following violent demonstrations in Teheran, Iran, President Barack Obama said

> *The United States and the international community have been appalled and outraged by the threats, the beatings, and imprisonments of the last few days. I strongly condemn these unjust actions, and I join with the American people in mourning each and every innocent life that is lost.*

He then opened the floor to NBC's Chuck Todd, who asked

> *TODD: Mr. President, I want to follow up on Iran. You have avoided twice spelling out consequences. You've hinted that there would be, from the international community, if they continue to violate—you said violate these norms. You seem to hint that there are human rights violations taking place.*
>
> *THE PRESIDENT: I'm not hinting. I think that when a young woman gets shot on the street when she gets out of her car, that's a problem.*
>
> *TODD: Then why won't you spell out the consequences that the Iranian—*

THE PRESIDENT: Because I think, Chuck, that we don't know yet how this thing is going to play out. I know everybody here is on a 24-hour news cycle. I'm not.

TODD: But shouldn't—I mean, shouldn't the world and Iran—

THE PRESIDENT: Chuck, I answered—

TODD: —but shouldn't the Iranian regime know that there are consequences?

THE PRESIDENT: I answered the question, Chuck, which is that we don't yet know how this is going to play out. [1.1]

Another tense exchange occurred on March 1, 2013. In a press briefing following severe cuts made in the federal budget, President Obama said

None of this is necessary. It's happening because of a choice that Republicans in Congress have made. They've allowed these cuts to happen because they refuse to budge on closing a single wasteful loophole to help reduce the deficit.

He then opened the floor to the Associated Press's Julie Pace who asked

Thank you, Mr. President. How much responsibility do you feel like you bear for these cuts taking effect? And is the only way to offset them at this point for Republicans to bend on revenue, or do you see any alternatives?

In his response, Obama said

But what is true right now is that the Republicans have made a choice that maintaining an ironclad rule that we will not accept an extra dime's worth of revenue makes it very difficult for us to get any larger comprehensive deal. And that's a choice they're making. They're saying that it's more important to preserve these tax loopholes than it is to prevent these arbitrary cuts.

which prompted the reporter to repeat her question:

PACE: It sounds like you're saying that this is a Republican problem and not one that you bear any responsibility for.

THE PRESIDENT: Well, Julie, give me an example of what I might do.

PACE: I'm just trying to clarify your statement.

THE PRESIDENT: Well, no, but I'm trying to clarify the question. [1.2]

The President of the United States can dismiss Chuck Todd with, "I answered the question, Chuck!" or Julie Pace by turning her question back to her for an answer, but you do not have that luxury. In business, you must respond fully to your audience whether that person is a customer, an investor, or a manager.

To do that, you have to understand the reason business people ask challenging questions. Is it because they are mean-spirited? Perhaps. Is it because they want to test your mettle? Perhaps. More likely it is because when you are presenting your position, you are asking your opposite party or parties, your target audience, to change, which is just the case in almost every decisive communication in business—as well as in those other walks of life. Most human beings are resistant to change, and so they kick the tires.

You are the tires.

The most mission-critical of all business presentations is the initial public offering (IPO) road show, a form of communication I have had the privilege and opportunity to coach for nearly 600 companies, among them Cisco Systems, Intuit, Yahoo!, Dolby Laboratories, eBay, and most recently, Trulia, the successful real estate search engine company. In those road show pitches, presenters ask their investor audiences to change: to buy a stock that never existed. In fact, when a company offers shares to the public for the first time, the U.S. Securities and Exchange Commission mandates that they specifically state the risk in print. The offering company must make available a prospectus containing a boilerplate sentence that reads, "There has been no prior public market for the company's common stock." In other words, *caveat emptor*—or, "Invest at your own risk." As a result, when a company's executive teams take their presentations on the road, they are inevitably assaulted with challenging questions from their potential investors.

Although the stakes in an IPO road show are exceedingly high—in the tens or hundreds of millions of dollars—the character of the challenge is no different from that of potential customers considering a new product, potential partners considering a strategic relationship, pressured managers considering a request for additional expenditures, concerned citizens considering a dark horse candidate, a human resources manager considering a new employee, or even affluent contributors considering a donation to a nascent, not-for-profit cause.

The inherent challenge in these circumstances is compounded in presentation settings where the intensity level is raised by several additional factors:

- **Public exposure.** The risk of a mistake is magnified in large groups.
- **Group dynamics.** The more people in the audience, the more difficult it is to maintain control.
- **One against many.** Audiences have an affinity bond among themselves and apart from the presenter or speaker.

The result is open season on the lone figure spotlighted at the front of the room, who then becomes fair game for a volley of even more challenging questions.

How then, to level the playing field? How then, to give the presenter the weapons to withstand the attack?

The answer lies in the David versus Goliath match, in which a mere youth was able to defeat a mighty giant using only a stone from a slingshot. This biblical parable has numerous equivalents in military warfare. History abounds with examples in which small, outnumbered, under-equipped units were able to combat vastly superior forces by using adroit maneuvers and clever defenses. Remember the Alamo, but also remember Thermopylae, Masada, Agincourt, the Bastille, Stalingrad, the Battle of the Bulge, Iwo Jima, and the Six-Day War. All these legendary battles share one common denominator: leverage, or the use of agility to counter force.

▪▪■ Martial Arts

For our purposes, the most pertinent modern equivalent is martial arts, in which a skilled practitioner can compete with a superior opponent by using dexterity rather than might. Bruce Lee, a diminutive kick boxer, became an international star by virtue of his uncanny ability to prevail over multiple and mightier armed opponents using only his flying feet and hands. The martial arts, which evolved from Asian philosophy and religion, employ these six critical mental and physical skills:

- Concentration
- Self-defense
- Balance
- Agility
- Preparation
- Self-control

I've translated each of these martial arts skills into a set of best practices that you can apply in your mission-critical encounters so that you can succeed in your challenging exchanges. Deploy these pivotal dynamics against a sea of troubles and, by opposing, you can end them.

This overarching objective can be stated in one word: control. Although it will take 200 pages to provide you with the details, when you are confronted with tough questions, you can control

- The question
- Your answer
- The questioner
- The audience
- The time
- Yourself

■■ Effective Management Perceived

A synonym for the verb "control" is "manage." Therefore, the subliminal perception of a well-handled question is *Effective Management*. Of course, no one in your target audience is going to conclude that you are a good manager just because you fielded a tough question effectively. That's a stretch. But the converse proves the point. If your response to a challenging question is defensive or contentious, you lose credibility—and with it the likelihood of attaining your objective in the interchange. If your response is prompt, assured, and to the point, you will be far more likely to emerge unscathed, if not fully victorious.

The causal relationship between behavior and perception was eloquently expressed by David Bellet, the former Chairman of Crown Advisors International, one of Wall Street's most successful long-term investment firms. As an early backer of many successful companies, among them Hewlett-Packard, Sony, and Intel, Bellet was solicited to invest almost daily. In response, he often fired challenging questions at his petitioners.

"When I ask questions," he said, "I don't really have to have the full answer because I can't know the subject as well as the presenter. What I look for is whether the presenter has thought about the question, been candid, thorough, and direct and how the presenter handles himself or herself under stress; if that person has the passion of 'fire in the belly' and can stand tall in the line of fire."

▬■ Baptism Under Fire

I, too, was once in the business of asking tough questions. Before becoming a presentation coach for those nearly 600 IPO road shows, as well as for thousands of other presentations ranging from raising private capital to launching products, seeking partnerships, and requisitioning budget approvals, I spent a decade as a news and public affairs producer at WCBS-TV in New York. As a student of the classical art of drama and with the full knowledge that conflict creates drama, I became an expert at asking challenging questions.

My baptism under fire came early in my tenure at CBS when I was assigned to be the Associate Producer of a documentary series called *Eye on New York*, whose host was the then recently hired Mike Wallace. Although *60 Minutes*, Mike's magnum opus, had not yet begun, he came to CBS largely on the strength of the reputation he had developed on another New York television station as an aggressive interrogator on a series called *Night Beat*. Mike had regularly bombarded his *Night Beat* guests with tough questions and was intent on maintaining his inquisitorial reputation at CBS. He fully expected his Associate Producer to provide him with live ammunition for his firepower. Heaven help me when I did not.

Fortunately, I survived Mike's slings and arrows by learning how to devise tough questions. In the process, I also learned how to handle those same questions. This book is a compilation of those techniques, seasoned and battle-tested for 25 years in business with my corporate clients.

Expanding upon David Bellet's observation, the objective of this book is not so much to show you how to respond with the right answers as it is to show you how to establish a positive perception with your audiences by giving them the confidence that you can manage adversity, stay the course, and stay in control.

2

The Critical Dynamics of Q&A

To fully appreciate the importance of control in handling Q&A sessions, we must start by looking at the consequences of lack of control. Most presenters react to tough questions in one of two ways: They become either defensive or contentious.

▬■ Defensive

On April 19, 2007, Alberto Gonzales, the then U.S. Attorney General, testified before the Senate Judiciary Committee as part of its investigation of his Justice Department's firing of eight federal prosecutors. According to a *Washington Post* report of the hearings, Gonzales used the phrase, "I don't recall," and its variants ("I have no recollection," "I have no memory") 64 times during his testimony!

The *Post* report went on to describe Gonzales' defensive behavior that accompanied his testimony: "For much of the very long day, the attorney general responded like a child caught in a lie. He shifted his feet under the table, balled his hands into fists and occasionally pointed at his questioners." [2.1]

Another example of defensive behavior came from New York Congressman Anthony Weiner. On Memorial Day weekend in 2011, a conservative blog reported that Weiner had tweeted a lewd photo of himself to a young woman in Washington. The story went viral, becoming what *Forbes* called, "the perfect storm for news coverage, involving social media, political scandal, and fun word play given Rep. Weiner's last name." [2.2]

At first, Weiner dismissed the whole matter as a prank and that someone had hacked his Twitter account, but the perfect storm would not subside. In an effort to defend himself Weiner consented to a number of television interviews, but the more he defended himself, the more defensive he appeared. When MSNBC's Rachel Maddow asked whether the photo was of him, Weiner responded:

THE CRITICAL DYNAMICS OF Q&A

The photograph doesn't look familiar to me but a lot of people who have been looking at this stuff on our behalf are cautioning me that—you know—stuff gets manipulated. Stuff gets—you know—you can—you can— you can change a photograph, you can manipulate a photograph, you can doctor a photograph. And so, I don't want to say with certitude it maybe didn't start out being a photograph of mine and now looks as something different, or maybe it was something that was from another account that got sent to me. I—I don't—I can't say for sure. I don't want to say with certitude and I'm not trying to be evasive. I just don't know. [2.3]

■■■ Contentious

Different people react differently to challenging questions. Although Gonzales and Weiner reacted defensively, others go in the opposite direction and become contentious. One of the most combative men ever to enter the political arena is H. Ross Perot, the billionaire businessman with a reputation for cantankerousness.

In 1992, Perot ran for president as an independent candidate and, although he conducted an aggressive campaign, lost to Bill Clinton. The following year, ever the gadfly, Perot opposed the Clinton-backed North American Free Trade Agreement (NAFTA). His opposition culminated on the night of November 9, 1993, when Perot engaged then Vice President Al Gore in a rancorous debate on Larry King's television program.

In the heat of battle, Perot launched into the subject of lobbying.

You know what the problem is, folks? It's foreign lobbyists...are wreckin' this whole thing. Right here, Time Magazine *just says it all, it says "In spite of Clinton's protests, the influence-peddling machine in Washington is back in high gear." The headline,* Time Magazine*: "A Lobbyist's Paradise."*

Gore tried to interject:

I'd like to respond to that.

Larry King tried to allow Gore to speak:

All right, let him respond.

Perot barreled ahead, his forefinger wagging at the camera—and at the audience:

We are being sold out by foreign lobbyists. We've got 33 of them working on this in the biggest lobbying effort in the history of our country to ram NAFTA down your throat.

Gore tried to interject again:

I'd like to respond...

But Perot had one more salvo:

That's the bad news. The good news is it ain't working.

Having made his point, Perot leaned forward to the camera, smiled smugly, and returned the floor to his opponent:

I'll turn it over to the others.

Larry King made the hand-off:

OK, Ross.

Gore took his turn:

OK, thank you. One of President Clinton's first acts in office was to put limits on the lobbyists and new ethics laws, and we're working for lobby law reform right now. But, you know, we had a little conversation about this earlier, but every dollar that's been spent for NAFTA has been publicly disclosed. We don't know yet...tomorrow...perhaps tomorrow we'll see, but the reason why...and I say this respectfully because I served in the Congress and I don't know of any single individual who lobbied the Congress more than you did, or people in your behalf did, to get tax breaks for your companies. And it's legal.

Perot bristled and shot back:

You're lying! You're lying now!

"You're lying!" is as contentious as a statement can be. True to form, Perot showed his belligerent colors.

The Vice President looked incredulous:

You didn't lobby the Ways and Means Committee for tax breaks for yourself and your companies?

Perot stiffened:

What do you have in mind? What are you talking about?

Gore said matter-of-factly:

Well, it's been written about extensively and again, there's nothing illegal about it.

Perot sputtered, disdainfully:

Well that's not the point! I mean, what are you talking about?

With utter calm, Gore replied:

Lobbying the Congress. You know a lot about it.

Now Perot was livid. He glowered at Gore and insisted:

I mean, spell it out, spell it out!

Gore pressed his case:

You didn't lobby the Ways and Means Committee? You didn't have people lobbying the Ways and Means Committee for tax breaks?

Contemptuous, Perot stood his ground:

What are you talking about?

Gore tried to clarify:

In the 1970s...

Perot pressed back:

Well, keep going.

Now Gore sat up, looked his opponent straight in the eye, and asked his most direct challenging question:

Well, did you or did you did you not? I mean, it's not...

His back against the wall, Perot fought back:

Well, you're so general I can't pin it down! [2.4]

Ross Perot's bristling behavior is matched by Arizona Senator John McCain, a self-described maverick who prides himself for his cantankerous demeanor. When he ran for President in 2008, McCain called his campaign bus, "The Straight Talk Express." His caustic remarks often gave him the upper hand on the floor of the Senate and in his frequent jousts with the media. But the approach backfired when he debated Barack Obama in a town hall debate on October 7, 2008:

> *McCAIN: By the way, my friends, I know you grow a little weary with this back-and-forth. It was an energy bill on the floor of the Senate loaded down with goodies, billions for the oil companies, and it was sponsored by Bush and Cheney.*
> *You know who voted for it? You might never know. That one. [2.5]*

As McCain said "That one," he gestured disdainfully at Obama seated behind him without looking at him.

Kathleen Parker, the conservative columnist for the *Washington Post* wrote that "there's a reason it was so stunning in the moment. I…don't think it was racist, as some have argued. But it was objectifying. 'That one' isn't the same as 'that man.' One is an object; the other is a person. A human being. 'That one' has a dehumanizing effect and one is right to recoil." [2.6]

One final example of contentious behavior comes from the same Anthony Weiner who provided the earlier example of defensiveness. Pardon the play on words, but Weiner worked both sides of the Q&A aisle.

On July 29, 2010, a little more than a year before the scandal about the tweeted lewd photo, Weiner gave an impassioned speech on the floor of the House of Representatives. The staunch Democrat vehemently denounced a Republican majority vote to defeat a bill that would have provided aid to the victims of the 9/11 attacks:

> *We see it in the United States Senate every single day, where members say, "We want amendments, we want debates, we want amendments, but we're still a 'No.'" And then we stand up and say, "Oh, if we only had a different process we'd vote 'Yes.'" You vote "Yes" if you believe "Yes." You vote in favor of something if you believe it's the right thing. If you believe it's the wrong thing you vote "No." We are following a procedure…*

At this point in his tirade, another person in the House chamber, off camera, attempted to interject a question or statement. Weiner went ballistic, shouting and gesticulating angrily:

> *I will not yield to the gentleman and the gentleman will observe regular order—the gentleman will observe regular order! [2.7]*

The adjectives *defensive* and *contentious* are synonyms for "fight or flight," the human body's instinctive reaction to stress. In each of the cases just presented, the response to tough questions was fight or flight. The contentious Ross Perot, John McCain, and Anthony Weiner behaved as pugnaciously as bare-knuckled street brawlers; the defensive Alberto Gonzales and Anthony Weiner behaved like men desperately trying to flee the hot seat.

■■■ Presenter Behavior/Audience Perception

Any presenter or speaker who exhibits negative behavior produces a negative impression on the audience.

Alberto Gonzales' negative behavior produced a very negative impression on Tom Coburn, a Republican member of the Senate Judiciary Committee, who told the Attorney General: "'It was handled incompetently. The communication was atrocious…You ought to suffer the consequences that these others have suffered, and I believe that the best way to put this behind us is your resignation.'" [2.8]

Four months later, the embattled Gonzales submitted his resignation letter to President George W. Bush. [2.9]

It took only three weeks after the Twitter posting for the embattled Anthony Weiner to resign. [2.10]

Ross Perot's behavior on the *Larry King Live* program also had a profound effect. Figure 2.1 shows the results of the public opinion polls taken on the day before and the day after the debate.

In the 48 hours between the two polls, the only factor with any impact on the NAFTA issue was the debate between the chief proponent and the chief opponent on the *Larry King Live* program. Ross Perot's contentious behavior swung the undecided respondents against his cause.

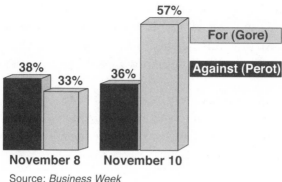

Source: *Business Week*

▲ **FIGURE 2.1** *1993 NAFTA public opinion polls (reprinted by permission of* Business Week*).*

Two months after the debate, the U.S. Congress ratified NAFTA.

As a footnote to the impact of the debate, that episode of the *Larry King Live* series became the highest-rated program on cable television, a distinction it held for 13 years forward until *Monday Night Football* moved from over-the-air on ABC to ESPN.

▬▬■ The Six-Million-Dollar Q&A

One other example of negative behavior in response to challenging questions comes from that most challenging of all business communications, an IPO road show. Historically, when companies go public, the chief executives go on the road to pitch investors, and they travel to about a dozen cities over a period of two weeks, having up to 10 meetings a day for a total of 60 to 80 iterations of their road show presentation in each of those meetings.

One particular company had a successful business when they went public. They had accumulated 16 consecutive quarters of profitability. Theirs was a simple business concept: a software product that they sold directly into the retail market. The CEO, having made many presentations over the years to his consumer constituency, as well as to his industry peers, was a proficient presenter. At the start of the road show, the anticipated price range of the company's offering was $9 to $11 per share.

However, having presented primarily to receptive audiences, the CEO was unaccustomed to the tough questions that investors ask. Every time his potential investors challenged him, he responded with halting and uncertain answers.

After the road show, the opening price of the company's stock was $9 per share, the bottom of the offering range. Given the 3 million shares offered, the swing cost the company $6 million.

■■■ The NetRoadshow Factor

Q&A became even more mission critical in 2005 when the Securities and Exchange Commission mandated that companies offering stock to the public for the first time must make their road show presentation available online. Since then, every company makes video recordings of their executive management teams delivering their pitches and posts them, along with slideshows that accompany their narratives, on a website called netroadshow.com or its companion site retailroadshow.com (see Figure 2.2).

Therefore, by the time the executives of any offering company arrive at the meeting, most of the potential investors have already seen the pitch.

▲ **FIGURE 2.2** *NetRoadshow page (courtesy of NetRoadshow).*

Despite this wide access, the executive teams still make that grueling two-week tour because no investor will make a decision—based on a canned presentation alone—to buy up to a 10% tranche of an offering in the tens of millions of dollars. Investors want to meet the executives in person, press the flesh, look them in the eye, and interact with them directly. As a result, many of the meetings are not presentations at all, but intense Q&A sessions.

All of this harkens back to David Bellet's observation that investors are looking to see how a presenter stands up in the line of fire. Investors kick the tires to see how the management responds to adversity. Audiences kick tires to assess a presenter's mettle. Employers kick the tires of prospective employees to test their grit. In all these challenging exchanges, the presenter must exhibit positive behavior that creates a positive impression on the audience.

The first steps in learning how to behave effectively begin in the next chapter.

CHAPTER

3

Effective
Management
Implemented

▪▪▪ Worst-Case Scenario

Soldiers prepare for battle by conducting realistic maneuvers. Athletes prepare for competition by practicing with extra resistance or weights. Politicians prepare for debates by staging mock rehearsals with skilled stand-ins for their opponents. Supreme Court nominees prepare for their Senate Judiciary confirmation hearings by participating in mock sessions called "Murder Boards."

In preparing yourself to step into the line of fire when you open the floor to questions, assume the worst-case scenario: that all the questions you will be asked will be the most hostile possible— like those Mike Wallace fired at thousands of interviewees. If you can learn to handle that caliber of ammunition, you can learn to handle any question.

To raise the bar even further, let's assume that all your Q&A sessions will be conducted in large groups: the one-against-many dynamic. If you can survive those odds, you will be able to handle any question in any encounter, even one-to-one.

▪▪▪ Maximum Control in Groups

In most large group settings with 50 or more people in the audience, the presenter usually has a microphone, and the audience does not, which allows the presenter to deliver the full presentation uninterrupted. In this situation, the audience members usually hold their questions to the end. In small group settings, the opposite is true: Because of the informality and immediacy, the audience members freely ask questions at any time during the presentation, which usually turns the presentation into discussion. Nevertheless, in each setting, the presenter must always remain in control whenever a question is asked.

Let's start with the large group. At the end of a presentation, the presenter opens the floor to questions and then proceeds to step through the following inflection points (see Figure 3.1):

- Open the floor
- Recognize the questioner
- Yield the floor
- Retake the floor
- Provide an answer

After the answer, the cycle starts again and continues on to another member of the audience, and then another, in recurrent clockwise cycles.

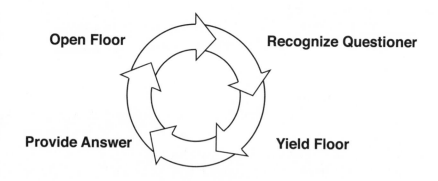

Open Floor   **Recognize Questioner**

Provide Answer   **Yield Floor**

Retake Floor

▲ **FIGURE 3.1** *The Q&A cycle.*

▇▇■ The Q&A Cycle

Each of the steps in the cycle provides an opportunity to exercise control, and as you will see, those control measures are applicable to both large and small groups.

Open the Floor

Control the Time

When the presentation is done and you open the floor to questions, say, "We have time for only a few questions," or "We've got to catch a plane and don't have time for questions," or "We'll take all your questions in the breakout session," or "We'll be here for the rest of the afternoon to answer any questions you might have." It doesn't matter which option you chose. It matters that you state it up front and set the time expectations for your audience.

Then, as you get closer to the end of your Q&A session, fulfill your forecast by starting to count down: "Three more questions," "Two more," "One more," "Last question." Exert time management.

Control the Traffic

In what is a carryover from grade school, people in large groups usually raise their hands when they want to speak. That practice often carries forward in small groups. You can leverage that custom by raising your own hand when you start your Q&A session, implicitly inviting your audience members to raise theirs if they want to be recognized. When you open the floor, raise your hand and say, "Who has a question?" Your audience might launch right into questions without raising their hands, but you have a better chance if you establish this signal. Of course, this tactic is only appropriate in audiences where there is a peer relationship. Do not raise your hand if you are presenting to a group of potential investors or the Board of Directors.

In small groups, all bets are off. The informality of these sessions makes these suggestions null and void. In these cases, skip the first step and advance to the second.

Recognize the Questioner

Let's say three hands go up at some point either during or after your presentation. You get to choose which one to recognize. Use an open hand and do not point. All too often, presenters or speakers point to indicate their selection. This is perfectly acceptable in a bakery, but not in presentations. To avoid this unconscious tendency in your Q&A sessions, exercise a simple arithmetic equation: one plus three. Extend your forefinger, but roll out your other three fingers to create an open palm. Receive your questioners openly.

In presidential press conferences, tradition has it that the president addresses a few select reporters by name. You are not the president of the United States. You might be the president of your company, but you do not have the same privileges.

For instance, let's say you know John, but you don't know the man seated behind him. You recognize John first and call him by name. Then you recognize the man behind John and call him "Sir." The second man will feel the outsider.

Take the same circumstances but reverse the order. The first person you recognize is the man behind John, and you call him "Sir." No problem. Then you recognize John, and call him "Sir," too. Because you know John, and John knows you know him, you will not offend him.

The rule of thumb is: *If you know the name of every person in the room, call everyone by name. If you do not know the name of every person in the room, call no one by name.* If you call the names of only selected people, you run the risk of implying favoritism at least and collusion at worst.

Yield the Floor

Let's say that you recognize the gentleman or the woman in the middle of the room, and you now yield the floor to that person.

This is a very big moment. Your motor has been running at full speed delivering your presentation. During that entire time, that audience member's motor has been idle. You step on the brakes and screech to a halt, and that person's motor suddenly lurches into motion.

Do most people ask questions in a clear, crisp, and succinct manner? No; most of the time their questions are long and rambling. Why? Is it because your audiences are not very bright? No, it's because they have just taken in a great deal of new information and are still processing it. Furthermore, this mental activity occurs largely in the right hemisphere of the brain, which processes data in a non-linear, random order. The questioner, suddenly aware that everyone in the room is watching—we've all been there—becomes self-conscious and nervous. That person's ill-formed thoughts then come tumbling out in a disjointed, run-on statement, which may or may not even take the form of a question.

In the meantime, you, who are very knowledgeable and clear about your own subject matter, receive your questioner's discursive statement in a heightened state of alertness and perceive it as confused. All these diverse and counteracting dynamics can produce dramatic results.

▄▄■ How to Lose Your Audience in Five Seconds Flat

Try this exercise: Stand up and ask a seated colleague to ask you a long, rambling question on any subject. It can be about the weather, the news, or your business. Ask that person to keep their eyes fixed on you as they ramble. Shortly after they start, thrust your hands into your pockets and settle back onto one foot. Watch what happens. Usually, the person's ramble will start to sputter and slow down. Ask the person how your slouch felt to them, and they will very likely say that it felt as if you weren't listening.

I do this exercise in my private sessions with my clients, and they tell me, "You look like you weren't interested," "You were bored," "You were being impatient," or "You could care less."

When a presenter sends that kind of message to an audience, the effect can be devastating. That moment arrests all forward progress. All communication stops. You cannot even contemplate proceeding to the next two vital inflection points in the Q&A cycle (please refer to Figure 3.1): Retake the floor and provide the answer. In fact, we will defer consideration of these points until you learn what to do when you yield the floor: Listen effectively.

4

You're Not Listening!

Falstaff: "It is the disease of not listening, the malady of not marking, that I am troubled withal."

2 Henry IV, Act I, Scene ii
by William Shakespeare

Breathes there a man or woman who has not accused or been accused by their significant other of not listening? Highly doubtful. The opprobrium of not listening ranks high among the causes of failure in human communication; it spans interpersonal, business, political, and even international relations. To the perpetrators of what troubled Falstaff, listening is merely a matter of waiting one's turn to speak.

For the *reductio ad absurdum* of this universal truth, think of a time when you were in a restaurant where you have given your waiter explicit instructions to exclude garlic, bacon, or butter from your meal, only to have your meal arrive reeking of garlic, littered with bacon bits, or swimming in butter. The waiter will suffer, at best, a return trip to the kitchen or, at worst, a diminished tip.

Notch the stakes up to interpersonal communications, and the consequence can be an argument at best or a severe strain on the relationship at worst. In business, the consequence can be failure to close the deal, gain approval, or get the investment. Remember the example of the CEO whose halting responses to tough questions resulted in a lower share price of his company's initial public offering?

Why would anyone in a mission-critical communication setting risk such a fate? The paradoxical reason is that when most people in business—being results-driven by nature *and* nurture *and* culture—see a problem, they immediately try to find a solution. That same ingrained habit makes them respond to questions with quick answers. With good intentions and seemingly efficient behavior, they rush to bring an open question to resolution. To further their cause, they often retain professional communication consultants, public relations advisors, or media coaches to help them by preparing a long list of tough queries and a parallel list of canned answers in what is known as "Rude Q&A."

A more apt name is "Wrong Q&A," for a couple of reasons. First, people don't ask questions as written sentences; they ramble. Moreover, if you formulate your answer before you fully understand the key issue in the question, your prepared answer might not match. This very likely will propel you into a desperate mental scramble to find a match and result in a wrong answer. Your wrong answer will then result in an audience reaction that virtually shouts, "You're *not* listening!"

A dramatic case in point of this vicious cycle occurred on October 15, 1992, in the second presidential debate among George H. W. Bush, the incumbent president, and his challengers, Bill Clinton, the then-governor of Arkansas, and H. Ross Perot, the billionaire businessman with a reputation for belligerence. The leading contenders were each dealing with challenging issues: President Bush with a struggling national economy and Governor Clinton with recent revelations of an extramarital affair, marijuana use, and his participation in anti-Vietnam war protests.

All three candidates gathered in the Robbins Field House at the University of Richmond in Virginia to engage in the first-ever town hall format in which they had to respond to questions posed by ordinary citizens. Carole Simpson, an ABC Television journalist, was the moderator, and one of the citizens she recognized was a twenty-six-year-old black woman named Marisa Hall.

A runner from the Commission on Presidential Debates (the non-partisan group that organizes the matches) brought a hand microphone to Marisa Hall, who asked:

> Yes. *How has the national debt personally affected each of your lives?*

As she was asking her question, Bush looked at his wristwatch, as shown in Figure 4.1.

▲ **FIGURE 4.1** *George H. W. Bush looking at his watch during a presidential debate.*

Marisa Hall continued:

> *...And if it hasn't, how can you honestly find a cure for the economic problems of the common people if you have no experience in what's ailing them?*

Bush began his answer:

> *Well, I think the national debt affects everybody.*

Her microphone still open, Marisa Hall said:

> *You personally.*

She said "You personally." George H. W. Bush, said "everybody." He wasn't listening. Stopped in his tracks, he tried to recover:

> *...Obviously it has a lot to do with interest rates—*

The moderator interjected:

She's saying, "you personally."

Marisa Hall tried to clarify her question:

You, on a personal basis—how has it affected you?

Carole Simpson tried to help:

Has it affected you personally?

Bush replied:

I'm sure it has. I love my grandchildren—

Marisa Hall's soft voice, amplified by the live microphone, rose above the exchange to resound through the Robbins Field House public address system, out along a vast network of coaxial cables to television transmitters, across the United States into millions of television receivers and into banks of video tape recorders that captured her word for posterity:

How?

This was the second time she asked the question, and Bush still didn't understand. He tried to answer again:

I want to think that they're going to be able to afford an education. I think that that's an important part of being a parent. If the question—maybe I—get it wrong. Are you suggesting that if somebody has means that the national debt doesn't affect them?

Three times and he still didn't have it. The young woman tried to clarify again, her voice rising ever so slightly:

What I'm saying is—

Bush finally gave up:

> *I'm not sure I get—help me with the question and I'll try*
> *to answer it.*

It took four attempts until he admitted that he didn't understand her question. The young woman tried to help:

> *Well, I've had friends that have been laid off from jobs.*

Despite a fretful expression on his face, the president tried to sound attentive:

> *Yeah.*

The young woman continued:

> *I know people who cannot afford to pay the mortgage on*
> *their homes, their car payment. I have personal problems*
> *with the national debt. But how has it affected you and if*
> *you have no experience in it, how can you help us, if you*
> *don't know what we're feeling?*

Bush still seemed puzzled, so Carole Simpson intervened again:

> *I think she means more the recession—the economic*
> *problems today the country faces rather than the deficit.*

Now clearer, the President launched into his answer:

> *Well, listen, you ought to be in the White House for a*
> *day and hear what I hear and see what I see and read the*
> *mail I read and touch the people that I touch from time to*
> *time. I was in the Lomax AME Church. It's a black church*
> *just outside of Washington, D.C. And I read in the bulletin*
> *about teenage pregnancies, about the difficulties that*
> *families are having to make ends meet. I talk to parents. I*
> *mean, you've got to care. Everybody cares if people aren't*
> *doing well.*

His voice rising defensively, he continued:

> *But I don't think it's fair to say, you haven't had cancer. Therefore, you don't know what it's like. I don't think it's fair to say, you know, whatever it is, that if you haven't been hit by it personally. But everybody's affected by the debt because of the tremendous interest that goes into paying on that debt everything's more expensive. Everything comes out of your pocket and my pocket. So it's that.*
>
> *But I think in terms of the recession, of course you feel it when you're president of the U.S. And that's why I'm trying to do something about it by stimulating the export, vesting more, better education systems.*
>
> *Thank you. I'm glad you clarified it. [4.1]*

George H. W. Bush's long, circuitous route to answer the young woman's question created the distinct impression that he wasn't listening or that he was completely out of touch. This negative impression compounded and exacerbated a similar impression he had made just eight months before this painful exchange. In February of 1992, the president paid a visit to the National Grocers Association convention in Orlando, Florida, where he was shown a common electronic bar code scanner. According to reports in several newspapers, he seemed amazed to learn about a product that had been in supermarkets since the 1980s.

James Carville, Clinton's campaign manager, seized upon the bar code scanner incident and magnified it to major proportions with his notorious slogan, "It's the economy, stupid." To a nation mired in an economic downturn, Marisa Hall's question was right on target. It was also to become the point of no return for George H. W. Bush, as the public opinion polls show in Figure 4.2.

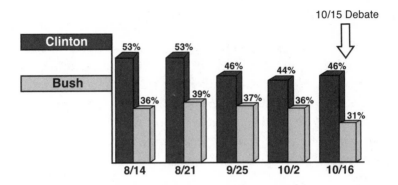

▲ **FIGURE 4.2** *1992 Presidential public opinion polls.*

Politicians consider the day after the last major party nominating convention to be the formal start of presidential election campaigns. In 1992, when the Republican Convention ended (8/14), Clinton had surged into a 17-point lead over Bush for a variety of reasons, among them the troubled economy. Moreover, because that year the Democratic Convention preceded the Republican Convention, Clinton enjoyed the benefits of national media exposure. In the political trade, this is known as "bounce."

The week following the Republican Convention (8/21), Bush, having had his own media exposure, got his own bounce and closed Clinton's lead to 14 points. Over the next several weeks, (9/25 through 10/2), Bush's poll numbers held steady. During that same period, Ross Perot became a candidate, and Clinton's numbers dropped precipitously to only an 8-point lead. The campaign became a horse race. But then on October 15, Marisa Hall asked her fateful question in the town hall debate. The very next day, the poll numbers for Bush and Clinton began to diverge and continued in those directions until election day in November.

Never again would such an incident occur in presidential debates. Four years later in 1996, the candidates eliminated follow-on questions *de facto*. President Bill Clinton and Senator Bob Dole, two highly skilled debaters, were such good listeners that, in their town hall format, none of the citizens asked a single follow-on question. Both candidates always got the key issue and threaded the needle with their answers from their respective points of view.

Four years later, in 2000, the possibility of follow-on questions was eliminated *de jure*. When George H. W. Bush's son, George W. Bush, participated in the same open town hall format (against then Vice President Al Gore), the rules changed. At the start of that year's debate, the moderator, the veteran PBS newsman, Jim Lehrer, announced:

> *The audience participants are bound by the following rule. They shall not ask follow-up questions or otherwise participate in the extended discussion. And the questioner's microphone will be turned off after he or she completes asking the question. Those are the rules. [4.2]*

Four years later, in 2004, when president George W. Bush committed to another town hall debate format (this time against Senator John F. Kerry), his representatives set even more rigorous ground rules in advance. The moderator, Charles Gibson of *ABC News*, announced them at the start of the debate on October 8, 2004:

> *[E]arlier today, each audience member gave me two questions on cards like this, one they'd like to ask the president, the other they'd like to ask the senator. I have selected the questions to be asked and the order. No one has seen the final list of questions but me, certainly not the candidates. No audience member knows if he or she will be called upon. Audience microphones will be turned off after a question is asked. [4.3]*

In 1992, Marisa Hall's microphone was left open for all the world to hear her resounding "How?" As decisive and as devastating as the events resulting from her follow-on question appear, they were actually even worse for George H. W. Bush.

Yes, he did look at his wristwatch as she asked her question and sent the message that he wasn't listening, but after he looked at his watch he had another 55 seconds in which to formulate a better response. That interval was occupied by Ross Perot's answer. Marisa Hall's question was addressed to all three men, and Perot went first.

As soon as the young woman finished asking her question, Perot volunteered:

May I answer that?

The moderator approved:

Well, Mr. Perot—yes, of course.

Perot asked:

Who do you want to start with?

Marisa Hall explained:

My question is for each of you, so—

Perot took the floor:

It caused me to disrupt my private life and my business to get involved in this activity. That's how much I care about it. And believe me, if you knew my family and if you knew the private life I have, you would agree in a minute that that's a whole lot more fun than getting involved in politics.

But I have lived the American dream. I came from very modest background. Nobody's been luckier than I've been, all the way across the spectrum, and the greatest riches of all are my wife and children. That's true of any family. But I want all the children—I want these young people up here to be able to start with nothing but an idea like I did and build a business. But they've got to have a strong basic economy and if you're in debt, it's like having a ball and chain around you. I just figure, as lucky as I've been, I owe it to them and I owe it to the future generations and on a very personal basis, I owe it to my children and grandchildren. [4.4]

Despite Perot's succinct, empathic, and relevant answer, George H. W. Bush took his turn next with an answer that was far enough off target to invite interruption—three interruptions—and create the distinct perception that he *wasn't listening*.

It got still worse for George H. W. Bush. Following his rambling answer and awkward exchange with Marisa Hall, Bill Clinton's turn came. As the President headed back to his stool, the challenger rose from his and walked toward Marisa Hall, addressing her directly:

Tell me how it's affected you again.

His approach put Marisa Hall at a momentary loss for words:

Um—

Continuing toward her, Clinton prodded her memory:

You know people who've lost their jobs and lost their homes?

Marisa Hall agreed:

Well, yeah, uh-huh. [4.5]

"Well, yeah, uh-huh." She could just as well have said, "You *were* listening!" In that one pivotal moment, Bill Clinton became the complete opposite of George H. W. Bush. In that one pivotal moment, the die was cast for the dark horse challenger's victory at the expense of the incumbent.

There was also the matter of Clinton's words. One month after President Bush's moment with the bar code scanner had worked against him, Clinton faced a challenging moment of his own that he turned into an advantage. On March 26, 1992, Clinton appeared at a political fundraiser in New York. During his speech, Bob Rafsky, a member of an organization called AIDS Coalition to

Unleash Power, or ACT UP, interrupted Clinton and accused him of not doing enough to combat AIDS. Clinton departed from his speech to respond to Rafsky, and the exchange became heated. For a short while, the two went toe-to-toe, but Clinton finally put an end to the quarrel when he said, "I feel your pain." [4.6]

"I feel your pain." Early on in his run for office, Bill Clinton saw and understood the power of those four words. They were to become the leitmotif of his campaign and the engine he would ride to victory and the White House. The underlying implication in those words is not only "I heard you," but also, and more importantly, "I care about you."

As soon as Bill Clinton heard Marisa Hall say, "Well, yeah, uh-huh," he picked up the ball and ran with it.

> *Well, I've been governor of a small state for 12 years. I'll tell you how it's affected me. Every year Congress and the president sign laws that make us do more things and gives us less money to do it with.*

Now Clinton shifted into overdrive. He made his entire point of view identical to Marisa Hall's.

> *...I see people in my state, middle class people—their taxes have gone up in Washington and their services have gone down while the wealthy have gotten tax cuts.*
>
> *I have seen what's happened in this last 4 years when— in my state, when people lose their jobs there's a good chance I'll know them by their names. When a factory closes, I know the people who ran it. When the businesses go bankrupt, I know them.*
>
> *And I've been out here for 13 months meeting in meetings just like this ever since October, with people like you all over America...*

When Clinton said, "people like you," Marisa Hall nodded her head silently. She could just as well have lifted her microphone again and said, "You were listening!"

Just then, the live television broadcast cut to a close two-shot of Clinton and Marisa Hall, and captured her assenting nod.

Bill Clinton rolled on:

> ...*people that have lost their jobs, lost their livelihood, lost their health insurance.*
> *What I want you to understand is the national debt is not the only cause of that.*

Even though Carole Simpson had, during George H. W. Bush's answer, tactfully and tacitly corrected Marisa Hall's confusion of the national debt with the recession, Clinton took the opportunity to repeat the young woman's original words—*the national debt*—and, in so doing, further validated her. Then he answered her:

> ...*It is because America has not invested in its people. It is because we have not grown. It is because we've had 12 years of trickle-down economics. We've gone from first to twelfth in the world in wages. We've had 4 years where we've produced no private sector jobs. Most people are working harder for less money than they were making ten years ago.*
> *It is because we are in the grip of a failed economic theory. And this decision you're about to make better be about what kind of economic theory you want, not just people saying I'm going to go fix it but what are we going to do? I think [what] we have to do is invest in American jobs, American education, control American health care costs and bring the American people together again. [4.7]*

The chain reaction of repercussions that nullified George H. W. Bush's bid for re-election can be traced back to a single pivotal moment: providing the wrong answer to a question. That moment, as reported by the *Washington Post*, was marked "at Virginia Commonwealth University [where] 105 uncommitted voters watched the proceedings with 'debate meters' in hand, instantly recording when they had a positive or negative reaction to what the candidates were saying. Bush scored one of his two most negative responses of the evening with his answer to Hall." [4.8]

George H. W. Bush's fumbled answer, which set in motion an avalanche that brought down the house of the 41st Presidency, was a classic example of the critical blunder: "Ready, Fire, Aim!" He pulled the trigger before he had the target in his sights.

Although very few people get the opportunity to try to win the Presidency of the United States, everyone who tries to win in business and, in fact, everyone who tries to win in any endeavor by seeking the concurrence of other people, must avoid the fatal mistake of not listening. The remedy is a seemingly simple but deceptively counter-intuitive two-step solution:

■ Listen correctly.
■ Answer properly.

In the next chapter, you will learn the first step with a skill called Active Listening—and how close the first President Bush came to getting Marisa Hall's question right. In the succeeding chapters, you will learn how to answer properly and by Chapter 8, "Topspin in Action," learn how George H. W. Bush might have answered her differently.

This delay in providing you with prescriptive instruction about answers is intentional. It is specifically designed to drive a deep wedge between the tough question and your answer. When you learn just what to do in that gap, you will be able to avoid the all-too-common malady that troubled Falstaff, will trouble your audience, and ultimately will trouble your cause.

5

Active Listening

(Martial Art: Concentration)

Let me tell you a story...about the Japanese Zen master who received a university professor who came to inquire about Zen. It was obvious to the master from the start of the conversation that the professor was not so much interested in learning about Zen as he was in impressing the master with his own opinions and knowledge. The master listened patiently and finally suggested that they have tea. The master poured his visitor's cup full and then kept pouring.

The professor watched the cup overflowing until he could no longer restrain himself. "The cup is overfull, no more will go in!"

"Like this cup," the master said, "you are full of your own opinions and speculations. How can I show you Zen unless you first empty your cup?"

Zen in the Martial Arts [5.1]

IN THE LINE OF FIRE

Let's flash forward to the end of your next mission-critical presentation and assume that it was the performance of a lifetime. Everything went perfectly: Your narrative was eloquent, your Microsoft PowerPoint slides were illustrative, your delivery was authoritative, and your audience watched and listened in spellbound admiration.

Now you Open the Floor to questions and you call on the gentleman in the middle of the room. This is the moment of suspended animation we left at the end of Chapter 3, "Effective Management Implemented," when you Yielded the Floor.

The man starts asking a question, but it sounds like Greek to you. You can tell that it has something to do with the material you just delivered, but the point of his rambling question is unclear to you. Being a results-driven person, you are eager to provide an answer.

That is just what happened to George H. W. Bush. He wanted to provide an answer to Marisa Hall, except that the answer he gave was not to the question she asked. She did not ask about his grandchildren or teenage pregnancies, nor did she ask about a black church just outside of Washington, D.C. What *did* she want to know? What should President Bush have done instead of answering?

Heed the advice of the Zen master: *Empty your cup.* Empty your mind of all your thoughts so that you can fill it instead with those of the questioner. *Concentrate.*

Concentration is essential in every activity in the human experience, particularly in sports, and even more particularly in the martial arts where mortality is at stake. This was vividly illustrated in the 2003 film, *The Last Samurai*, in which Tom Cruise played an American soldier who, in his quest to become a Samurai warrior, learns to fight with a lethal sword. Director

Edward Zwick captured Cruise's concentration by shooting the swordfight in wide angles first; and then, at a pivotal moment he replayed the same scene from Cruise's point of view in close-up. When Cruise observes the same pivotal moment, he watches his opponent's actions in extreme slow motion, sees a fault, and understands how to defeat him. His concentration brings him victory.

During your Q&A session, concentrate on your questioner's pivotal words as if in slow motion. This will be difficult to do in the heat of battle and under the glare of attention of the audience. The solution: Step on the brakes. Avoid the "Ready, Fire, Aim!" trap. *Resist thinking of the answer and instead listen for the key issue. Concentrate.* Listen for the one or two words that identify the essence of the question, the heart of the matter.

Unfortunately, the key issue comes all wrapped up in a large knotty ball. One of the strands of that ball is misinformation. Marisa Hall confused the national debt and the recession, and Carole Simpson, the moderator, tried to clarify by defining the terms:

> *I think she means more the recession—the economic problems today the country faces rather than the deficit.*

Despite Simpson's well-meaning effort, she took the discussion off on a tangent and away from the central issue.

One of the other strands wrapping and masking Marisa Hall's question was her emotion:

> *Well, I've had friends that have been laid off from jobs...I know people who cannot afford to pay the mortgage on their homes, their car payment. [5.2]*

Other strands that can obscure the key issues in any question include:

- Nonlinear right-brain thinking
- Unprepared extemporaneity
- Anxiety about standing up in front of an audience

As a result of these factors, most questions come tumbling out helter-skelter, wrapping a dense thicket of strands around the key issue, producing a stream of jumbled words that is completely unclear to the presenter.

The challenge for you, as it was for President Bush, is to unwrap the ball. Peel away all the strands until you can see the Roman Column.

▪▪▪ The Roman Column

In the glory days of the Roman Empire, around 100 BCE, the great Roman orators, such as Cicero, spoke in the Forum for hours on end without a note in their hands. The invention of paper in China was still a couple of hundred years away. Instead, those orators used the stately marble columns of the Roman Forum as memory triggers. As the orators strode around the Forum delivering their rhetoric, they stopped at various columns and discoursed eloquently on particular themes. Each column represented the focal point for a cluster of related ideas. Before you Open the Floor to questions about your mission-critical presentation, you must find your own Roman Columns, find your key issues. (For a more complete discussion of Roman Columns and the techniques to define them, please see my other Pearson book, *Presenting to Win: The Art of Telling Your Story*.)

What was the Roman Column in Marisa Hall's question?

Please note that the balance of this page is blank. This is for you to stop and think, or to look back at the transcript of the question in the previous chapter and try to identify her key issue.

The operative word in Marisa Hall's question was *how*—the very word that had stopped George H. W. Bush in his tracks during the debate. She wanted to know how each of the candidates could solve the nation's economic problems given that they had no personal experience with them. She also had another *how*: how those economic problems affected them. But this second *how*, although posed first, was subordinate to her primary concern: whether these three candidates—two of whom were multimillionaires and one a career politician with two terms as governor—could provide solutions to the country's economic problems when they clearly had none of their own. This constitutes a *double* Roman Column: the first being the impact of the economic problems on each man and the second, their ability to deliver solutions.

Marisa Hall asked her question twice, stating "affect" each time, and referring to solutions first as "a cure" and then as "help." Her first time was while George H. W. Bush was looking at his watch:

> *How has the national debt personally affected each of your lives? And if it hasn't, how can you honestly find a cure for the economic problems of the common people if you have no experience in what's ailing them?*

The second time was when, after four failed attempts, the President asked her to help him by clarifying her question, and she responded:

> *But how has it affected you and if you have no experience in it, how can you help us, if you don't know what we're feeling?*

Did you get the Roman Columns? Don't worry if you didn't. I show the video of that exchange to my private clients, then pause the clip and ask them the same question I asked you. Many people have seen that video, but only about a quarter of them get it right. The rest get sidetracked by the discussion of the national debt and recession. They think that the Roman Column is *only* about how the national debt or recession has *affected* the candidates personally. This is close, but no cigar. The cigar is: How can you *help* us?

George H. W. Bush actually touched on Marisa Hall's main concern *twice* during his exchange with her. First, as he struggled to understand her question:

> *Are you suggesting that if somebody has means that the national debt doesn't affect them?*

But he couched his question about her question so defensively and negatively that he backed himself into a corner and could not extricate himself. Instead, he simply gave up and asked the young woman to restate her question. After she did, he circled around the ability issue again during his rambling answer:

> *I don't think it's fair to say, you haven't had cancer. Therefore, you don't know [what it's like]. I don't think it's fair to say, you know, whatever it is, that if you haven't been hit by it personally.*

The negative tone of his words—three "don'ts" and two "haven'ts"—put him into reverse gear, unable to turn his answer positive.

As a matter of fact, none of the three candidates dealt specifically with the question of his *ability*. They all went directly to their solutions; an acceptable shift given that Marisa Hall was seeking "a cure for the economic problems of the common people."

Bill Clinton heard both of Marisa's concerns loud and clear. He addressed each Roman Column, beginning his answer with the first: how the "national debt" affected him:

> *Well, I've been governor of a small state for 12 years. I'll tell you how it's affected me....*

And concluded his answer with the second: his solutions, articulated by the action verb "do"—four ways:

> *I think [what] we have to do is invest in American jobs, American education, control American health care costs and bring the American people together again.*

Ross Perot also heard Marisa clearly. He began his answer with her first issue: how the "national debt" affected him:

> *It caused me to disrupt my private life and my business to get involved in this activity. That's how much I care about it....*

And concluded his answer with the second: his solution:

> *—I want these young people up here to be able to start with nothing but an idea like I did and build a business. But they've got to have a strong basic economy....*

Actually, President Bush also offered his solutions at the very end of his answer:

> *But I think in terms of the recession, of course you feel it when you're president of the U.S. And that's why I'm trying to do something about it by stimulating the export, vesting more, better education systems.*

But his "do" words came at the tail end of his one minute and ten second answer, after his false start, four fumbled attempts, two interruptions, a tangential discussion, and a digressive ramble, by which time it was far too late. Clinton and Perot did not get to their solutions until the ends of their answers either, but each of them started his answer in the first person, thereby empathizing with Marisa Hall's concern. George H. W. Bush began his answer by going universal:

> *Well, I think the national debt affects everybody.*

By generalizing, the President, in effect, distanced himself from the economic problems. Worse, in doing so, he ignored one of Marisa Hall's Roman Columns, which evoked her fateful follow-on question and, in turn, sent the message that he wasn't listening. Imagine if George H. W. Bush had *begun* his answer with his last words:

> *I'm trying to do something about it by stimulating the export, vesting more, better education systems.*

When Bill Clinton came bounding off his stool toward Marisa Hall to ask her, "Tell me how it's *affected* you again?" he evoked her "Well, yeah, uh-huh," response. And when, three sentences later, he began his answer with, "I'll tell you how it's *affected* me..." he sent the message that he had listened.

Emulate Bill Clinton in your Q&A sessions: Listen carefully to your audience and evoke your own equivalent of "Well, yeah, uh-huh."

▪▪▪ Subvocalization

A very simple method to enable your Active Listening is *subvocalization*. Speak to yourself under your breath. Silently say the words that represent the Roman Column. "He's asking about *competition*," or "She's concerned about the *cost*," or "He wants to know about the *timing*."

As a matter of fact, President Bush used a hybrid form of subvocalization in his third attempt to answer Marisa Hall's question. Speaking aloud, he asked rhetorically:

> *Are you suggesting that if somebody has means that the national debt doesn't affect them?*

That was only the subordinate half of what she was suggesting, so he got no "Well, yeah, uh-huh," as Bill Clinton did. Instead of continuing on to clarify the key issue, President Bush gave up:

I'm not sure I get—help me with the question and I'll try to answer it.

The lesson for you is to listen carefully for the Roman Column and subvocalize to help formulate it. Think of the Key Words, the one or two nouns or verbs central to the questioner's issue, hear them in your mind, but do *not* answer until you are certain you understand.

▬▪ Visual Listening

Another vital part of Active Listening is the physical expression of your attentiveness. Remember the exercise in Chapter 3 where you saw the negative effect of merely relaxing into a slouch while listening silently? Avoid this trap by keeping all the elements of your outward appearance as focused on the person asking the question as your inner workings are focused on processing his or her words.

- **Balanced stance.** Distribute your weight evenly on both your feet.
- **Eye Connect.** Lock your eyes on the questioner as if you are a laser beam.
- **Head nods.** Show that you are in receive mode.
- **Voice assent.** Utter a few "Uh-huhs" or "Mm-hmms."
- **Steady fingers.** Don't let your fingers twiddle or fidget. If they do, a simple remedy is to squeeze the tips of your fingers in a short burst of pressure. This will drain the tension out of your hands.

Now let's go back to the moment when you've Yielded the Floor to the man in the middle of the room. Let's say that you've listened carefully, you've subvocalized intently, you've "Mm-hmmed" several times, and you've nodded your head repeatedly, but you *still* don't understand.

▦ ▪ ...You *Still* Don't Understand

It was at this point that George H. W. Bush made the fatal mistake of moving past the point of not understanding and, at that moment, became guilty of the Zen master's accusation, "You are full of your own opinions and speculations." The President speculated. He asked the young woman a question about a question:

> *Are you suggesting that if somebody has means that the national debt doesn't affect them?*

Because he was off the mark, Marisa Hall started to correct him:

> *What I'm saying is— [5.3]*

Her voice rose on the word *saying*, indicating her frustration and therefore echoing—as well as validating—James Carville's "It's the economy, stupid" slogan. A close cousin of Marisa Hall's vocal exasperation is the more common, "Well, what I'm *really* asking..." in which the voice rises on the word *really*. That irritable emphasis in the questioner's voice radiates out through the audience like wildfire. In the case of George H. W. Bush, the audience was the millions of people watching the debate and, ultimately, the majority of the electorate.

When some presenters don't understand the question, they make the mistake of trying to interpret. They say, "Let me see if I have this right..." which gives the questioner the opportunity to say, "No, you don't have it right!" The message is, *"You weren't listening!"*

Some presenters make the other mistake, known as the deafness ruse. They hear the question. Everyone else in the room hears the question, but the presenter, in an innocent tone of voice, says, "Could you repeat the question?" *The pretense is transparent.*

Other presenters go all the way to the end of their answer to a question that they didn't understand in the first place, and they see the narrowed eyes of the questioner glowering back at them. If the presenter, as far too many presenters do, then says, "Does that answer your question?" or its close cousin, "Is what you're asking…?" the questioner has the opportunity to say, "No." The message is, *"You weren't listening!"*

Remove all of these statements from your vocabulary:

- "Let me see if I have this right…"
- "Could you repeat the question?"
- "Does that answer your question?"
- "Is what you're asking…?"

If you do not *completely* understand the question—and completely means 100%, not 99.999%—imagine a bold red line between you and your audience. Do *not* cross the line. Do *not* Retake the Floor. Do *not* answer. Do *not* interpret. Psychiatrists have difficulty interpreting veiled meanings. And as the Zen master counsels, do *not* speculate.

Do *not* Retake the Floor. Instead, Return to Sender by saying, "I'm sorry, I didn't follow, would you mind restating the question?" In doing so, *you* take the responsibility for not understanding, rather than pointing out that the questioner asked an unintelligible question.

What will the questioner do?

He or she will rethink the question and then restate it in simpler terms. And you are off the hook. The key here again is the foundation of Active Listening: Do *not* answer until you fully comprehend the Roman Column.

■■■ Yards After Catch

In North American football, an important measure of success is a statistic called "Yards After Catch," or YAC. It refers to receivers who catch a pass for a gain of yards and then run for additional yards. Superior receivers are able to add many yards *after* they catch a pass. The not-so-superior receivers, in their desire to become superior, often take their eyes off the ball and start to run *before* they catch the ball. They then fail to make the catch *and* the yards. The play fails.

The YAC analogy applies here. Do not take a step into your answer until your hands are on the ball, until you fully grasp the Roman Column.

You can get the Roman Column on your own with Active Listening, or you can get it by asking the questioner to clarify. Either way, with the key issue firmly in your mind, you are now—and *only* now—finally ready to move forward in the control cycle to Retake the Floor.

6

Retake the Floor

(Martial Art: Self-Defense)

Become one with the opponent, like an image reflected in the mirror.

Ittosai Sensei Kenpo-Sho
(Teacher Ittosai Sword Manual)
By Kotoda Yahei Toshida
(1716) [6.1]

When your Q&A session moves from Yield the Floor to Retake the Floor, the shift in dynamics presents another opportunity for you to exercise control. The energy in the room shifts away from the questioner and back to you.

Let's return our focus to that moment after you have Opened the Floor to the gentleman in the middle of the room. He has asked his long, rambling question and you, either on your own, or through his restatement, now fully grasp the Roman Column in his question. Being a results-driven person, you are eager to provide him with an answer, but suppose the gentleman's question was challenging: "Wait a minute! You tell me that your product is going to save us money, and then you give me a sticker shock price that's twice as much as your competition asks! That's outrageous! Where do you get off charging so much?"

Then suppose the answer you give to this very irate person is, "When you consider the total cost of ownership of our solution, you'll see that it will cost you less in the long run."

You would then be telling your potential buyer that he is wrong. After all, the clear inference in his question was that you are charging too much, and the clear inference in your answer was that you are *not* charging too much.

That irate gentleman would then perceive you as contentious—similar to the public's perception of Ross Perot when he responded to Al Gore in the NAFTA debate by snarling, "You're lying!" For you, that perception is highly unlikely to induce your potential customer to give you a purchase order.

Another approach, widely considered conventional wisdom, is to repeat the question. However, if after you were asked, "Where do you get off charging so much?" you were to say, "Where do we get off charging so much?" you would validate the inference that you are overcharging. Your potential buyer would then perceive you as having admitted guilt. Or in the words made popular by comedian Jon Stewart, "Nailed it!"

What's worse, when you answer, you would most likely start out defensively: "When you consider the total cost of ownership...." In essence, you would be carrying forward a negative balance.

Therefore, when you get a challenging question, do *not* answer and do *not* repeat; instead, *paraphrase*.

■■■ Paraphrase

The prefix "para" is used to mean *beside* or *near*, as in *parallel*. This prefix occurs in words such as *paralegal*, *paramedical*, *parapsychology*, and *paramilitary*. All of these terms refer to alternate but correlative forms of the root words: *legal*, *medical*, *psychology*, and *military*. So a paraphrase is a restatement of a text or passage in another form or other word.

By paraphrasing challenging questions in your Q&A session, you deflect the challenge and *control* the meaning. Paraphrasing is distinctly different from restating or rephrasing because the prefix "re" means "again." The word *again* implies repetition, and repetition implies carrying forward the negative inference in the challenging question. A negative statement creates a negative perception. To create a paraphrase of the original question, begin with an interrogative word, such as

- "What...?"
- "Why...?"
- "How...?"

Then conclude your paraphrase with a question mark. These beginning and ending points then serve to bracket the centerpiece of the original question: the Roman Column.

Please note that the paraphrase is a reconfiguration of the original question and not a question about the original question. Asking a question about a question, as George H. W. Bush learned so painfully when he speculated, "Are you suggesting…?" is a tactic doomed to failure. Asking a question about a question implies that you weren't listening and, worse, gives control back to the questioner.

Answering a question with a question is also doomed to fail. An evasive device that has inexplicably gained favor in some quarters of sales training is to respond to a question by asking, "Why do you ask?" This tactic is perceived as ducking the issue and produces nothing but frustration and irritation in the asker. Irritation in the audience produces failure for the presenter.

A good paraphrase simply incorporates the words of the original question and retains the Roman Column. The paraphrase differs from a question in that the voice drops at the end of the sentence, as opposed to a question in which the voice rises inquisitively.

Now, let's look at the original question again: "Wait a minute! You tell me that your product is going to save us money, and then you give me a sticker shock price that's twice as much as your competition asks! That's outrageous! Where do you get off charging so much?"

What is the Roman Column in the question? The balance of this page is left blank for you to analyze the question.

If you said "overcharging," "high price," "expensive," or "costly," you would be focusing on the outer wrappings of the knotty ball...or the questioner's feeling or emotion about the price of your product.

The Roman Column is simply "price." That is center of the ball, free of any other tangled strands. That, as Sensei Ittosai counsels, is a reflection of your opponent's image in a mirror.

Now incorporate the word *price* within a paraphrase.

- Why have we chosen this price point?
- How did we arrive at the price?

Notice that when you strip the charged words, *sticker shock, twice as much, outrageous,* and *so much,* from the original question, you neutralize the hostility. Then, when you begin your answer, you will only have to address the price itself and not whether it is too high or too low.

By becoming one with your opponent in the paraphrase, you level the playing field. This is the essence of self-defense in the martial arts: By using agility to counter force, the engagement then proceeds as a contest between equals.

When you paraphrase in Q&A, you can proceed to answer the question your questioner asked without having to deal with any latent hostility. Your questioner cannot help but concur that you have identified the issue, and therefore that person will not say, with exasperation, "What I'm *really* asking...." Instead, that person will nod in agreement and release you to move ahead with your answer.

The head nod from the questioner is completely involuntary. In my private coaching sessions with my clients, I engage them in an exercise in which they fire tough questions at one another. If the person who is asked the question paraphrases correctly, the person who asked the question invariably nods in agreement. If the paraphrase is wrong, the asker does not nod. In fact, the wrong paraphrase often produces a frown or a shake of the head. When the paraphrase is correct, the asker nods. The asker *always* nods even though the exercise is a simulation and even though the participants are peers or colleagues and not adversaries.

Let's look at another hostile question: "There are dozens of little start-ups doing exactly what you're doing! Then there are all those big guys, with their entrenched market share. It's a jungle out there, and you're only just getting off the ground! What on earth makes you think that you can survive?"

What is the Roman Column? Decide before you turn the page.

I hope you didn't say "survive." Figure 6.1 shows why not.

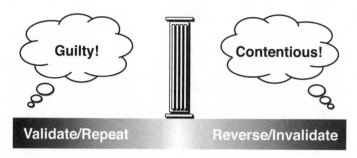

▲ **FIGURE 6.1** *Paraphrase positioning.*

Consider the light area in the center of the horizontal bar as the cool zone and the outer dark areas as the danger zones. Your objective is to position the Roman Column in the cool zone.

If you were to *repeat* the challenging question, "What on earth makes me think that we can survive?" you would land in the dark zone on the left because you would have *validated* that there is reasonable doubt that you could survive. Your audience would then perceive you as admitting *guilt*.

If you were to *reverse* the challenging question in your paraphrase, "Why will we succeed in this jungle?" you would land in the dark zone on the right because you would have *invalidated* the questioner's concern about your ability to survive. Your audience would then perceive you as being *contentious*.

The Roman Column is "compete." The paraphrase could be

- How do we compete?
- What is our competitive strategy?

Deal with only *how* you compete, not *whether* you can or cannot. Find the Roman Column and keep it within the cool zone. Use as few words as possible in your paraphrase. Confine those words to neutral nouns and verbs. Avoid adjectives and adverbs. Less is more. Mirror your opponent and neutralize the hostile question.

Let's look at another challenging question: "You know that this is a male-dominated industry and that most of the buying decisions are made by the buddy system in smoke-filled back rooms. What makes you, a woman, think that you can penetrate that old-boy network?"

What is the Roman Column? Decide before you turn the page.

I hope you didn't say "sexism" or "chauvinism." If you did, you would be responding to the value or emotion, the outer wrappings of the knotty ball. The Roman Column is "capability," and the paraphrases are

- What are my *capabilities?*
- Am I *capable* of reaching decision makers?

Another version of this hostile question is, "You look like a kid! I doubt that you've been in this business very long. I've been in this industry since before you were born, and now you come in here and tell me how I should run my business. Where do you get off telling me what to do?"

The Roman Column is the same as the earlier example, "capability," not age. The paraphrases are

- What are my *capabilities* to offer you solutions?
- Am I *capable* of offering you solutions?

All the previous long, rambling, challenging questions can be reduced to three single words: *price, competition,* and *capability.* The paraphrase strips out the hostility in each of them. Also note that all the paraphrases are neutral questions, positioning you to move on to a positive answer. Contrast this approach to the negativity latent in George H. W. Bush's words when he retook the floor after Marisa Hall's question.

> *Are you suggesting that if somebody has means that the national debt doesn't affect them?*

Any answer after that would be defensive. Imagine if instead he had paraphrased by saying, "How can I help you?"

The answer that would follow that paraphrase would contain an action verb, and be about his ability to provide solutions in response to Marisa Hall's resounding, "How?"

The paraphrase positions you right in the middle of the cool zone, ready to move forward positively. You can use this very powerful technique to control other types of challenging questions.

▬▬■ Challenging Questions

Negative

"This is the age of mergers. Banks are consolidating. Airlines and pharmaceutical companies are joining forces. Everybody's throwing their lot in with others. Instead of going out there and trying to be the Lone Ranger, why don't you throw in your lot with one of the larger companies in your sector? You can either get acquired, merge, or partner."

What Is the Roman Column?

The subtext of the question is this: Why don't you do what the questioner thinks you should do instead of what you just got finished spending your entire presentation telling the audience what you are going to do, which is to go it *alone*, aspiring for market leadership.

The Roman Column is "independence."

If you, as presenter, spend any time dealing with "Why don't you?" questions, you will only invite more negative questions, and you'll be swatting flies all day. Instead, turn the negative into a positive by addressing *only* why you are doing what you said you'd be doing in the presentation in the first place. The paraphrase is, "Why are we pursuing market leadership on our own?"

Irrelevant

"How come your logo doesn't have a space between the two words?"

This kind of question usually results in a smile, a snicker, or a frown from the presenter, each of which represents disdain to the questioner. When you're presenting, there is no such thing as an irrelevant question. Every question from every audience member is relevant and appropriate. If they ask it, you must answer it.

Inhibit the snicker or frown with the paraphrase, "What's behind our logo design?" or "Why did we chose this logo style?"

Multiple Questions

You will have no difficulty in handling related multiple questions such as: "How much did you spend on R&D last year? What percentage of your revenue did that represent? What is your R&D model going forward?" Any financial person could easily handle all three because they are related.

The difficulty comes when one of the multiple questions is from left field, another from right field, and another from the moon. What many presenters do in these circumstances is to dive into an answer for one of them and then lose track of the rest. At that point, the presenter often turns to the questioner and asks, "What was your other question?"

The audience perception: "You *weren't* listening!"

Don't burden yourself with having to remember someone else's right-brain, nonlinear thinking. Instead pick only *one* of the questions: the easiest, the hardest, the last, the first, the one that surprised you, or the one that you were expecting. Paraphrase the question, answer it, and then turn back to the person who asked and, in a *declarative* statement say, "You had another question!"

That person will either repeat the other question or say, "That's all right, you covered it." The latter response is common in Q&A sessions because most people can't remember their own right-brain ramble. Either way, you are off the hook and free to move forward to either answer the second question or move on to another questioner.

Another way to handle multiple questions is to write the questions as they are asked, showing respectful attentiveness to your audience. President Barack Obama used this technique in a press conference early in his first term.

Jeff Zeleny of the *New York Times* asked him, "During these first 100 days, what has surprised you the most about this office, enchanted you the most about serving in this office, humbled you the most and troubled you the most?"

The President immediately reached into his coat pocket, pulled out a pen and said, "Let me write this down," producing a wave of laughter from the crowd gathered in the East Room of the White House.

As Obama began writing, Zeleny began to restate his question, "Surprised...Troubled..."

Obama said, "I've got—what was the first one?"

Zeleny repeated, "Surprised."

Obama repeated, "Surprised."

Zeleny repeated, "Troubled."

Obama repeated, "Troubled."

Zeleny repeated, "Enchanted."

Obama repeated, "Enchanted." Then smiled and added, "Nice," evoking more laughter. [6.2]

Statement

The question that is not a question: "Your new solution appears to be very effective, but you've only just released it. You don't know if it has any kinks. I'd like to see it field-tested before I commit. It's not for us at this time."

If you were trying to land a sale for the early release of your promising new product, you certainly wouldn't want to leave the exchange at that point with no sale. Instead, turn the statement into a question by using the paraphrase, "Why adopt our new product now?" Your answer will then be about why your prospective customer wants to be the first kid on the block to enjoy the many benefits of your promising new product.

Presented Content

The final type of challenging question is the one asked about content you covered during your presentation. You've probably witnessed this common occurrence: A presenter delivers a thorough pitch about a new product, only to have a person in the audience ask a question about one of the product's main features. At an internal company meeting, this usually results in audible groans from the others in attendance. At an external meeting, the other audience members, being discrete, stifle their groans but think disdainfully about the person who asked it.

Presenters, being discrete and hopefully respectful, will also stifle groans but all too often begin their answers by saying, "As I said…." This seemingly innocuous phrase belies impatience with the questioner at best and condescension at worst. Worse still, are the presenters who begin their answers by saying, "Like I said…." This phrase is not only condescending but also poor grammar.

Instead, answer the question as if you've never covered the subject. Say, "Absolutely! Our new product performs this function better than any other product on the market!" You are then free to recap the main features of your new product. Resist the temptation, however, to mount the soap box and repeat the material in as much detail as you did in the presentation. Be succinct!

Avoiding back references produces three considerable benefits:

- **Reinforces** your selling points.
- **Validates**, rather than invalidates, the questioner.
- Creates a **Positive Perception**. Everyone in the audience will have heard you cover the content asked about in the question—except the person whose smartphone vibrated, drawing his or her attention away from you. When the rest of the audience observes you react patiently, they perceive you as a person in control. Cool under fire. Grace under pressure—*Effective Management*.

One important footnote about avoiding back references: In my earlier book, *Presenting to Win: The Art of Telling Your Story*, I advocated back references as a powerful narrative technique to create continuity in any story. However, in the free fire zone of Q&A sessions, where the one-against-many dynamics are in force, the rules change. Therefore, use only forward references.

All the foregoing techniques for handling challenging questions share a least common denominator that brings us full circle back to the martial arts.

■■■ The Buffer

By reframing the inbound energy of challenging questions, the paraphrase acts as a Buffer or shock absorber by deflecting the negativity. Like the martial arts, the Buffer is the first line of self-defense. *By becoming one with the opponent*, the Buffer levels the playing field between unequal forces: one presenter and many audience members. Then, after the Buffer discharges the negative energy, the presenter regains balance and moves ahead. The Buffer allows you to

- **Neutralize** hostile questions
- **Turn** negative questions positive
- **Treat** seemingly irrelevant questions the same as any other
- **Manage** multiple questions efficiently
- **Convert** charged statements into questions
- **Handle** questions about presented material with equanimity

Buffers have a host of other benefits…

- **"I heard you!"** This is the sine qua non of any Q&A session. It tells your questioner—and the rest of the audience—that you listened.
- **Condense**. There is no need to carry forward the random ramble of your questioner.
- **Thinking time**. Always a valuable asset; especially when you are in the line of fire.
- **Verbalize**. Verbalization means speaking aloud the actual words in the presentation to crystallize them. When you Verbalize the Buffer, you clarify the Roman Column in your own mind. (You will find a more detailed discussion of this powerful technique in the section on how to prepare for Q&A in Chapter 9, "Preparation.")
- **Trigger the answer**. When your mind is clear on the Roman Column, your answer follows readily.
- **Audibility**. Everyone in the audience hears the question you will answer.

Given all these valuable benefits, Buffer all questions, even those that are not challenging, such as, "Could you please describe how you plan to market your company in this competitive environment?" However, if you were to paraphrase this question by saying, "Could I describe how we're planning to market our company in this competitive environment?" you would sound stilted. Buffer instead with another, shorter form…*Key Word Buffer*.

▰▰■ Key Word Buffer

When a question is not challenging, you can use the Key Word or Words that identify the Roman Column and roll those words into your answer. For example, "Our marketing plan includes…" and then proceed with your answer.

You also can use the Key Word Buffer technique for tough questions, like the opening salvo in this chapter: "Wait a minute! You tell me that your product is going to save us money, and then you give me a sticker shock price that's twice as much as your competition asks! That's outrageous! Where do you get off charging so much?"

The Key Word Buffer is, "Our *pricing* is based on…"

Or the second round salvo: "There are dozens of little start-ups doing exactly what you're doing! Then there are all those big guys with their entrenched market share. It's a jungle out there, and you're only just getting off the ground! What on earth makes you think that you can survive?"

The Key Word Buffer is, "The way we will *compete* is…"

Or the third round salvo: "You know that this is a male-dominated industry and that most of the buying decisions are made by the buddy system in smoke-filled back rooms. What makes you, a woman, think that you can penetrate that old boy network?"

The Key Word Buffer is, "My *capabilities* include…"

Now you have two types of Buffers. One is the paraphrase that restates the question, and the other is to state the Key Words and then continue on into your answer. Together they provide the many benefits you read about earlier. However, some presenters are not content with one Buffer. They feel the need to put a Buffer in front of the Buffer, otherwise known as a *Double Buffer*. In the section that follows, you'll find—and most likely recognize—a collection of the most common Double Buffers used in Q&A sessions, all of which are useless fillers at the very least or counterproductive at the worst.

▪▪▪ The Double Buffer

The most common Double Buffer is

▪ "The question is…"

You can use this Double Buffer once. You can use it twice. You can use it three times. But if you use it before every paraphrase, you will sound as if you're stalling for time.

Two other common stalls for time are

▪ "That was a good question."
▪ "I'm glad you asked that."

Presenters often resort to either of these Double Buffers as a delaying tactic in reaction to a challenging question that was, in fact, not good, nor are they glad to have been asked it.

On the other hand, suppose an audience member were to ask you a question that was good for you, such as, "All these new features in your product should allow us to get our product to market faster, right?" You could then gleefully use both Double Buffers: "That was a good question! I'm glad you asked that!" and then go on to extol the virtues of your new product features.

But then suppose the next audience member were to ask you, "Yes, but why do you charge so much for that product?" You would hardly say, "That was a bad question! I'm *not* glad you asked that!" That would be judging and favoring one audience member over the other.

Another common Double Buffer is

■ "What you're really asking…"

The implication of this phrase is that the questioner isn't capable of formulating the question correctly and that the presenter will charitably reformulate it—an insult to the audience member.

Another Double Buffer is

■ "If I understand your question…"

The implication of this Double Buffer is the fatal message, "I wasn't listening."

And the final common Double Buffer is

■ "The issue/concern is…"

If you use the word *concern* or *issue* when you Retake the Floor, you confirm that there is a concern or an issue between you and your audience. Worse still, you begin your answer by carrying forward a negative balance.

Delete all these Double Buffers from your vocabulary. If you want to use Double Buffers, insert the word *you*.

▄▄■ The Power of "You"

Insert a "you" in your Double Buffer before your paraphrase.

■ "You're asking…"
■ "You'd like to know…"
■ "Your question is…"

Contrast the first Double Buffer in this section with the last:
■ "The question is…"
■ "Your question is…"

The difference is one word, *you*, one of the most powerful in all human communication. A Google or Bing search of the Internet will produce millions of references to a study attributed to Yale University, ranking the most persuasive words in the English language. In all the rankings *you* leads the list—ahead of *love* and *money*.

A simpler proof of the power of *you* is that it is synonymous with a person's name. Further validation comes from the branding slogans of some of the world's most successful corporations:

- Are *you* ready? (Cisco Systems)
- *Your* potential, Our passion (Microsoft Corporation)
- Have it *your* way (Burger King)

Moreover, saying "you" establishes a direct interpersonal connection between you and your questioner. It creates Eye Connect between you and your questioner. *Eye Connect* is a more specific term than the conventional eye contact, which is usually done as a sweeping movement. Eye Connect means that when you look at a person in your audience, you stay connected with that person until you see him or her look back at you—until you feel the click of engagement. (For a complete discussion about Eye Connect, please see my book on delivery skills, *The Power Presenter: Technique, Style, and Strategy.*)

Here is why Eye Connect is important: If you were to look at your questioner during a long rambling question and then use the first Double Buffer, "*The* question is…" you would most likely turn to address the rest of the audience. This would abruptly break your Eye Connect with your questioner and make that person feel rudely abandoned.

If instead you were to use the second Double Buffer, "*Your* question is…" you would then remain in Eye Connect with your questioner and make that person feel attended. Moreover, you would then see how that person reacts to your Buffer. A frown would indicate that you didn't get it right, and a head nod would indicate that you did. When you get the head nod from your questioner—and only after you get the head nod—are you free to begin your answer.

The head nod is the equivalent of Marisa Hall's, "Well, yeah, uh-huh." The head nod is the ultimate benefit because it sends the message, "You heard me!" And remember, the head nod in response to an accurate Buffer is *involuntary*.

All the foregoing control measures, starting with the moment you Retake the Floor and continuing up to the moment when you are ready to provide an answer, can be summarized in what is known as the *Triple Fail-Safe*—three points of intervention to keep you from moving into the wrong answer.

▪▪▪ The Triple Fail-Safe

First Fail-Safe. Retake the Floor only after you have a complete grasp of the Roman Column in the question. This is the equivalent of the "Yards After Catch" football analogy you read about in the previous chapter on listening. Just as successful football receivers run for additional yards *only* when they have a complete grasp of the ball, move forward into your answer *only* when you have a complete grasp of the Roman Column in the question you were asked. If not, follow the same instructions the U.S. Postal Service stamps on mail with unclear addresses: "Return to Sender." Return the floor to the questioner by taking responsibility and saying, "I'm sorry, I didn't follow; would you mind restating the question?"

Second Fail-Safe. If you are certain that you have grasped the Roman Column, use the Key Word in your Buffer. During your Buffer, make Eye Connect with the questioner until you see that person's head nod, indicating that you have identified the Roman Column correctly. Move forward into your answer *only* after you see the head nod.

Third Fail-Safe. If, despite your best efforts, you get a frown instead of a nod, do not move forward into the answer. Instead, Return to Sender by saying, "I'm sorry, I didn't follow, would you mind restating the question?"

These three Fail-Safes, depicted in Figure 6.2, are check points that will keep you from rushing into the wrong answer. You will also avoid the dreaded "You're not listening!" perception or its close cousins, "That's not what I asked!" and "What I'm *really* asking…"

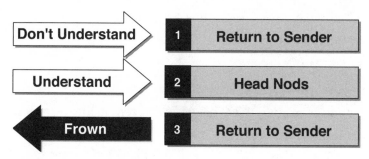

FIGURE 6.2   *The Triple Fail-Safe.*

Even with the Triple Fail-Safe, there is the possibility that, because the Roman Column straddles two related issues, you might not fully address both of them in your answer. At that point, the worst that can happen is that the questioner will ask you a follow-on question, "Yes, but what I'd also like to know is…" which is a lot milder than the dreaded, "You're not listening!" reaction.

Figure 6.3 is a graphical summary of this entire chapter: Build a bridge between a question and an answer with one of three Buffer options:

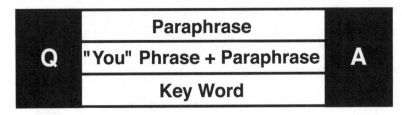

FIGURE 6.3 *Buffer summary.*

Paraphrase

A simple interrogative question.

- "Why have we chosen this *price* point?"
- "What are my *capabilities*?"
- "How do we *compete*?"

A "you" phrase before the paraphrase.

- "You're asking, 'Why have we chosen this price point?'"
- "Your question is, 'What are my *capabilities*?'"
- "You'd like to know how we *compete*."

Key Word Buffer.

- "Our *pricing* is based on..."
- "My *capabilities* include..."
- "The way we *compete* is..."

The first two options, the paraphrase and the paraphrase preceded by a "you" phrase, buy you thinking time. However, if you use these Buffers too often, you will sound stilted—even with the powerful "you" phrase. Although "you" has many benefits, too much of a good thing can become a bad thing. Starting every Buffer with "you" will make you sound like a hoot owl.

The third Buffer option, Key Words, gives you no thinking time at all. You must have a firm grasp on the ball before you take a single step. Make sure that the Roman Column is crystal clear in your mind when you utter the first word. However, when you respond without hesitation, with the Key Word embedded in your answer, you will appear very sharp and very much in control. The Key Word option is the most advanced form of Buffering.

An outstanding role model of Key Word Buffering is Colin Powell, one of the best presenters or speakers ever to command a podium. During his tenure as the U.S. Secretary of State, Mr. Powell held a press conference for foreign journalists on April 15, 2003, at the Foreign Press Center in Washington, D.C., shortly after the start of the Iraq War.

During the session, he fielded 11 questions, and never once did he use a paraphrase or a Double Buffer. In every case, he began his answer with the Key Word or Words inherent in the reporters' questions. Consider his challenge: Most of the foreign journalists spoke English as a second language, and so they formed their questions with unusual syntax and accents. Moreover, as professional journalists, they all tried to cram in multiple questions when their turns came.

In the following section from the transcript of the conference, we'll look at five of the reporters' questions and how, in each instance, General Powell promptly retook the floor with only the Key Word Buffer. Although his thorough answers continued well beyond his Key Word Buffer, in the interest of illustrating this powerful technique, we will examine only the front ends of the five questions—the inflection points at which he retook the floor and exercised control.

After a brief opening statement, Powell Opened the Floor.

I would be delighted to take your questions.

The first question came from a Russian man.

As the chief foreign policy advisor to U.S. President, do you think the U.N. is still relevant and important from the point of view of prevention of military conflicts, not only humanitarian assistance, and do you think the organization needs to be reformed?

What is the Key Word? Certainly not the last word, "reformed." If Powell were to deal with that issue, he would land in the dark danger zone on the left of Figure 6.1 because he would be validating the reporter's assertion that the United Nations is irrelevant and in need of reform. Any answer would then be an uphill fight to justify the U.N., which is the very opposite of the United States' stated supportive policy. Instead, the Secretary's first words upon retaking the floor were:

> *The U.N. remains an important organization.*

These Key Words served as a neutralizing Buffer that allowed Powell to go on to offer supporting evidence.

> *The President and other leaders in the coalition—Prime Minister Blair, President Aznar, Prime Minister Berlusconi, and many others, Prime Minister Howard of Australia— have all indicated that they believe the U.N. has a role to play as we go forward in the reconstruction and the rebuilding of Iraq.*

Powell's answer continued beyond this point, but let's move on to another question, this one from an Egyptian woman.

> *Thank you. Sir, the Israelis said that they presented to you their modification on the roadmap. Have you received anything from the other side, from the Palestinians? And is it still open for change? You have told us before that it is not negotiable. And now on the settlements, on the settlements, as part of the roadmap, eh?*

She was clearly rambling, so Powell tried to get her to clarify.

> *The what?*

She tried to explain herself.

> *On the settlements, which is part of the roadmap, we see the Israelis are—the activities of building settlements is really very high. We saw it on television. We saw reports...*

He tried to get her to finish by interjecting.

Thank you.

She continued,

So what is your remarks on the settlements?

What is the Key Word? Certainly not her last words, "the settlements." If Powell were to deal with that issue, he would he would again land in the dark danger zone on the left of Figure 6.1 because he would be validating the reporter's concern with an obstacle to the United States–sponsored peace efforts. Any answer would then focus on only a subordinate aspect of the U.S.'s larger initiative: the roadmap. Instead, his first words upon retaking the floor were:

With respect to the roadmap...

By using "the roadmap" as the Key Words rather than "the settlements," Powell created a neutralizing Buffer. This allowed him to move on to a substantive, rather than defensive, statement.

...the roadmap will be released to the parties after Mr. Abu Mazen is confirmed, and it will be the roadmap draft that was finished last December.

He continued his answer to her, but let's proceed to another question, this one from a Lebanese journalist.

Mr. Secretary, a lot of fears have been made about who is next. And some people believed to be close with the administration said that the regimes backing Cairo and in Saudi Arabia should be nervous right now. How do you address that point? And does the U.S. has a plan to spread a set of values at gunpoint, in your view, at this point?

"A plan to spread a set of values at gunpoint...." This question accused the United States of acting as a villainous bully, and Powell could not give credence to this charge! When he retook the floor, he immediately countered the accusation by applying the noted anti-drug slogan, "Just say, No!"

No, of course not.

This exchange is a variation of the common, "When did you stop beating your wife?" question. Such questions are false assumptions. You must counter every false assumption on the spot. Stop it in its tracks. Just say, "I never started beating my wife."

Neither Colin Powell, nor you, nor any presenter is under any obligation to respond to an accusation that is untrue in any other way than with a complete refutation. If you are attacked with a question that contains or implies an inaccuracy, do as Colin Powell did; skip the Buffer and come back immediately with a rebuttal.

After his rebuttal, Powell went on to support his position.

> *The President has spoken clearly about this, as recently as two days ago, over the weekend. We have concerns about Syria. We have let Syria know of our concerns. We also have concerns about some of the policies of Iran. We have made the Iranians fully aware of our concerns.*

He concluded with a firm restatement of his rebuttal.

But there is no list.

Colin Powell then had another accusation fired at him by a Mexican reporter, who asked:

> *Mr. Secretary, I have a question on Cuba. Can you give us an assessment of what is your advice to the countries that are near to both in terms of the human rights situation in Cuba, especially to Mexico that has been too close to the Cuban Government? And a quick second question. There is some countries that are calling the United States the "police of the world." Do you agree with that?*

"The police of the world...." This was another question that accused the United States of acting as a villainous bully! It was another false assumption and variation of the "When did you stop beating your wife?" question. Here again, Powell could not give any credence to this charge in his reply. However, because it was a double question, he fielded them in order, with Cuba first.

> *First of all, with respect to Cuba, it has always had a horrible human rights record. And rather than improving as we go into the twenty-first century, it's getting worse.*

Then, after a few supporting points about Cuba, Powell countered the accusation by just saying "No!"

> *With respect to the United States being the policemen of the world, we do not seek war, we do not look for wars, we do not need wars, we do not want wars.*

So it went with every other question in the press conference. Powell listened carefully and answered as each of the reporters challenged him with multiple questions, until he came to an Australian reporter.

> *Mr. Secretary, there seems to be some hopeful sounds coming out of your administration and North Korea on a settlement there. Do you think that there is likely to be a meeting soon between the administration and North Korea? And what sort of forum do you expect to attend? And how much do you think this is a flow-on from what happened in Iraq?*

Powell broke into a big grin.

> *Very good. You're trying to get it all at once, aren't you? [6.3]*

Powell then did go on to provide an answer about U.S. relations with North Korea. As with all the others, he began his answer with the Key Word Buffer and then went on to state his position consistent with United States policy.

So how did Colin Powell develop his expertise? In his most recent book, *It Worked for Me: In Life and Leadership*, he said that his education came on the job, but I had the rare privilege of meeting him and asking him the same question directly. His answer:

I first learned about presenting and answering questions in 1967 at Officer Training school in Fort Benning, Georgia, in an Instructor Training Course. They taught me to be sure to stand up straight, engage directly with the audience, and avoid affectation.

One of the most important lessons I learned about answering questions is to get to the point quickly. Leave them with a sound bite.

I also learned that there is no such thing as a stupid question, only stupid answers. The rest of the audience may be snickering at what they think is a stupid question, but the presenter must never react that way or talk down to a questioner.

Much of my learning about how to handle questions came from watching people who are really good at it. People like Ronald Reagan and Cap Weinberger (Powell served as a national security adviser in the Reagan administration and as a senior military aide to Secretary of Defense Caspar Weinberger.) I observed Reagan's and Weinberger's best practices and internalized them. My key takeaways were: show confidence, never let them see you sweat and always understand who your audience is.

Whenever I face the press, I know that I'm speaking not just to them, but to the American people. My relationship with the press is not adversarial. We have the same job: to inform the public. So I report what we've done—without giving away state secrets—and deliver what they want to know.

That same principle applies in business. It's always important to know your audience. Whenever I speak to a corporate organization, I research their track record, their stock performance, their industry, and I bring up that information in my presentation. I think about what my audience knows and what they want to know. I design my message and my answers to provide what they want.

Fielding questions in business is no different than fielding questions in the military and diplomatic sectors. I anticipate the questions that the audience is likely to ask and what my response will be. I have a random access memory and when I hear a question coming, I recognize it and deliver my prepared message in my response.

When I Retake the Floor, I often precede my answer with the words, "With respect to...." This simple technique has two benefits: It gives me a moment to think, and it shows respect to the audience. And that is the basis of all communication: care about your audience and show them respect. [6.4]

I'm pleased and proud to note that although I selected General Powell as a positive role model for Key Word Buffers, he validates all the other principles of my methodology, especially Audience Advocacy, the overarching concept that pervades every aspect of every presentation, and every form of communication.

To summarize the focus of this chapter, the Key Word Buffer technique provides the major benefits of the Buffer:

- Identifies the Roman Column
- Condenses the ramble
- Levels the playing field
- Tees up the answer

...all of which tees you up to learn how to answer in the next chapter.

CHAPTER

7

Provide the Answer

(Martial Art: Balance)

Yin and Yang are basic precepts in Chinese philosophy and refer to two opposing forces joining; the ultimate expression of balance.

Here we are about halfway into this book, and I have yet to provide you with advice on how to answer tough questions. This delay is fully intentional. Results-driven people, like you, tend to rush to answer too soon, which can produce the negative results that befell George H. W. Bush. During the delay, we've established three vital prerequisites to the answer:

- Listen for the Roman Column.
- Confirm the Roman Column in the Buffer.
- Look for the head nod from the questioner.

Conventional approaches to Q&A skills via public relations consultants, investor relations advisors, and media trainers merely list the potential questions and provide a parallel list of appropriate answers. This is a straightforward cause and effect or problem/solution approach, and is as necessary as balance is in the martial arts, but it skips the critical prerequisites. Only when you have fulfilled these vital requirements are you ready to move on to the final inflection point in the Q&A scenario, the answer.

Quid Pro Quo

The correct way to answer any question is governed by one overarching principal that goes back to the way to handle a seemingly irrelevant question: *If they ask it, you must answer it*. The same applies to *all* questions. After you Open the Floor—and yourself—to questions, your obligation is to respond. Other than questions to which you do not know the answer, you must reply to *any* question from *any* audience member. As in the martial arts, you must counterbalance one force with another; provide the complementary positive for the negative in the tough question: Provide the Yang for the Yin.

Furthermore, your answer must address the Roman Column in the question directly. Anything less will result in the "That's *not* what I asked!" or "What I'm *really* asking…" reaction, which is another way of saying, "You weren't listening!" The George H. W. Bush/Marisa Hall effect.

Any attempt to duck the issue in the answer will appear to be defensive or evasive. Remember how often Alberto Gonzales claimed memory failure or how evasive Anthony Weiner appeared when he said: "I—I can't say for sure. I don't want to say with certitude and I'm not trying to be evasive. I just don't know."

Alberto Gonzales' memory lapses and Anthony Weiner's dodges cost them their jobs. Two other unanswered questions produced unsuccessful results in the contest for the 2012 Republican presidential nomination.

During the campaign for the 2012 Republican presidential nomination, Texas Governor Rick Perry's candidacy flamed out because of his infamous brain lock in one televised debate and bungled statement in another. But what was largely overlooked in all the media attention was a moment in an October 18, 2011 debate on CNN, when moderator Anderson Cooper asked him this question:

> COOPER: *Governor Perry, the 14th Amendment allows anybody. A child of illegal immigrants who is born here is automatically an American citizen. Should that change?*
>
> PERRY: *Well, let me address Herman's issue that he just talked about.*
>
> COOPER: *Actually, I'd rather you answer that question.*
>
> PERRY: *I understand that. You get to ask the questions, I get to answer like I want to. [7.1]*

"I get to answer like I want to." Imagine a salesperson saying that to a customer, a mid-level manager to a senior executive, an executive to a board member, or a CEO to an investor. Meeting over. No deal.

Imagine saying that to your significant other. No comment.

Anderson Cooper called Rick Perry on it, "That's actually a response, that's not an answer...."

After Perry dropped out of the race, the other Republican candidates continued to engage in televised debates. In a later one, this exchange took place between Mitt Romney and CNN moderator John King:

> *KING: What is the biggest misconception about you in the public debate right now?*
>
> *ROMNEY: We've got to restore America's promise in this country where people know that with hard work and education, that they're going to be secure and prosperous and that their kids will have a brighter future than they've had. For that to happen, we're going to have to have dramatic fundamental change in Washington, D.C., we're going to have to create more jobs, have less debt, and shrink the size of the government. I'm the only person in this race—*
>
> *KING: Is there a misconception about you? The question is a misconception.*
>
> *ROMNEY: You know, you get to ask the questions want, I get to give the answers I want. [7.2]*

Governor Romney survived to become the 2012 Republican candidate, but he lost the election—and two out of three debates—with incumbent President Barack Obama. You'll read more about those debates in the following chapters, but the lesson here is that *you* must respond to all questions. The public has become inured to politicians not answering questions, but you do not have that option.

This is not to say that you should give away state secrets; you have every right to decline to answer on the basis of confidentiality, intellectual property, competitive data, or company or legal policy, but you must provide a rational reason for not answering—and "I get to answer like I want to" is not rational.

As in the martial arts, meet the key issue head on; provide a Yin for the Yang, quid pro quo.

▪▪▪ Manage the Answer

But meet the issue only head on. Resist the common temptation to introduce new, tangential information during your Q&A session. Far too many presenters veer off into another presentation *after* their presentation. Keep in mind that the only purpose in Opening the Floor to questions is to clarify the material *within* your presentation or speech. Proceed under the assumption that you have covered all your material thoroughly and that the Q&A period is an opportunity for the audience to get elaboration.

Under that same assumption, keep all your answers succinct. Resist the other common temptation to launch into oratory or to wax eloquent. A simple rule of thumb that will serve for most questions in most settings is to keep your answers to a maximum of 60 seconds.

▪▪▪ Anticipate

In advance of placing yourself in the line of fire, compile a list of the most challenging questions you might be asked. Compile only the questions and not the answers. Seek input for your list from as many resources as possible: your colleagues, your customers, your partners, your consultants and, if you can, even your competitors. When politicians prepare for debates, they use stand-ins for their opponents in their practice sessions. The next chapter covers practice and preparation in greater detail, but for now, be your own stand-in.

You know more about your own business premise than anyone else. Assemble the go-for-the-jugular questions, assume the worst-case scenarios. After your list is compiled, however, look it over carefully. You'll discover that, even if there are 100 tough questions, they all fall into groups of only a handful of red flag issues. You may also be surprised to discover that those red flag issues are the same in almost every industry. In my private practice, Power Presentations, Ltd., I consult for companies in information technology, life sciences, manufacturing, real estate, retail, restaurants, and even in the not-for-profit sector, and they all share the same universal red flag issues.

■■■ Recognize the Universal Issues

- **Management**: Do you have the right people? Is your team complete?
- **Competition**: How will you meet and beat the competition?
- **Growth**: How will you produce hockey stick results?
- **Price/Cost**: How did you choose that price point?
- **Contingencies**: What will you do if...?
- **Timing**: What's taken you so long? Why don't you wait?
- **Problems**: Questions about problems are usually phrased as, "What keeps you up at night?" Answer that question candidly, stating what does concern you, but then immediately follow with the actions you are taking to solve those problems.

- **Litigation**: As with problem questions, be candid about any litigious situations, but then immediately follow with the steps you are taking to protect and defend your ideas, or defer to legal counsel.

When you have identified these red flag issues as they relate to your business, develop a position statement for each of them. Craft this statement as if you were writing a press release for the media. This will take discussion and consultation with your key colleagues. When you have arrived at a consensus, it will merely be a matter of aligning the variation of the position statement with the variation of the issue in the challenging question. Do all your positioning during your preparation and not your presentation. Do all your thinking offline and not on your feet.

How to Handle Special Questions

Several different types of questions require special handling.

Tangential. In the previous chapter, you saw that there is no such thing as an irrelevant question. Or, as Colin Powell put it, "There is no such thing as a stupid question, only stupid answers." However, there is such thing as a tangential question, as in, "How come your logo doesn't have a space between the two words?" when the presentation is about stock performance. As with any question, a tangential question deserves an answer. Therefore, after you Buffer to keep from snickering or frowning at the questioner, you can either answer it directly, "We chose that as our branding style," or take it offline, "There are several reasons that I can share with you after the presentation."

False assumption. This is the familiar, "When did you stop beating your wife?" question, a close cousin of the two overstated accusations hurled at Colin Powell that "the U.S. has a plan to spread a set of values at gunpoint," and was acting as "the police of the world." Counter such false charges by just saying, "No."

Neither Colin Powell, nor you, nor any presenter is under any obligation to respond to an accusation that is untrue in any other way than with a complete refutation. Do as Colin Powell did; say, "Of course not."

Unknown. No audience member can reasonably expect you to be a walking encyclopedia, so if you do not know the answer to a question, particularly if it is about some minute detail, admit it to your questioner, but promise to get the answer to that person later. To support your intent, ask for a business card.

However, if the question is spot on to a central issue to your cause, you must respond directly and cannot duck it, or you will appear to be evasive.

President George W. Bush was confronted with such a situation on April 13, 2004. In the midst of a rare prime-time press conference about the controversial war in Iraq, a reporter asked:

> *In the last campaign, you were asked a question about the biggest mistake you'd made in your life, and you used to like to joke that it was trading Sammy Sosa. You've looked back before 9/11 for what mistakes might have been made. After 9/11, what would your biggest mistake be, would you say, and what lessons have you learned from it?*

President Bush replied:

> *I wish you would have given me this written question ahead of time, so I could plan for it. John, I'm sure historians will look back and say, gosh, he could have done it better this way, or that way. You know, I just—I'm sure something will pop into my head here in the midst of this press conference, with all the pressure of trying to come up with an answer, but it hadn't yet.*

He went on to reiterate the rationale for going into Afghanistan and Iraq and then concluded his answer with these words:

I hope I—I don't want to sound like I've made no mistakes. I'm confident I have. I just haven't—you just put me under the spot here, and maybe I'm not as quick on my feet as I should be in coming up with one. [7.3]

His response drew a great deal of attention in the media as being evasive. True to form, the media pursued the subject. Four months later, during an interview with the *New York Times*, a reporter asked the President:

At your last big press conference, you said that you couldn't think of any mistakes you had made. It's been about three or four months. Can you think of any now? It's been a long time.

This time, President Bush was able to joke about a mistake:

You mean other than having this interview? [7.4]

The subject was still alive two months later when President Bush met Senator Kerry to debate in a town hall format at Washington University in St. Louis, Missouri. One of the audience members, Linda Grabel, asked:

President Bush, during the last four years, you have made thousands of decisions that have affected millions of lives. Please give three instances in which you came to realize you had made a wrong decision, and what you did to correct it. Thank you.

President Bush answered:

I have made a lot of decisions, and some of them little, like appointments to boards you never heard of, and some of them big. And in a war, there's a lot of—there's a lot of tactical decisions that historians will look back and say: He shouldn't have done that. He shouldn't have made that decision. And I'll take responsibility for them. I'm human. But on the big questions, about whether or not we should have gone into Afghanistan, the big question about whether we should have removed somebody in Iraq, I'll stand by those decisions, because I think they're right.

That's really what you're—when they ask about the mistakes, that's what they're talking about. They're trying to say, "Did you make a mistake going into Iraq?" And the answer is, "Absolutely not." It was the right decision.

This time, the President provided quid pro quo to Linda Grabel's challenge by standing by his decision. He went on to further support his actions and then concluded his answer:

Now, you asked what mistakes. I made some mistakes in appointing people, but I'm not going to name them. I don't want to hurt their feelings on national TV. But history will look back, and I'm fully prepared to accept any mistakes that history judges to my administration, because the president makes the decisions, the president has to take the responsibility. [7.5]

The lesson here is that you must answer tough questions directly. You can do it lightly, with self-deprecating humor, be frank and 'fess up, stand your ground, or give a valid reason why you cannot answer, but you must address the issues that are prominent in the minds of your audience. Remember David Bellet's words from the Introduction: "What I look for is whether the presenter has thought about the question, been candid, thorough, and direct."

Confidential. If you get a question about classified or restricted material, and you say, "I'm not at liberty to reveal that," you will sound evasive. You will sound even more so if you say, "If I told you I'd have to kill you!"

Instead, provide a reason for your confidentiality. Attribute it to company policy, security, competitive data, legality, or privacy, and do it positively rather negatively. Rather than say, "We don't provide such confidential information," say, "It's our policy to provide only information previously mentioned in our press releases."

Senator John F. Kerry ran afoul of a confidential question during his 2004 quest for the presidency. Early in his campaign, Kerry claimed that foreign leaders backed his candidacy. Then, on March 14, at a town hall meeting in Pennsylvania, one man repeatedly asked the senator to identify which leaders, and Kerry repeatedly refused. The man continued to badger Kerry until in exasperation he blurted:

"That's not your business, it's mine." [7.6]

The immediate perception was that Kerry had something to hide. He could have changed that perception by giving a valid reason, such as, "That would be a breach of international courtesy."

Bill Clinton was faced with a question he could not answer during one of the most dramatic episodes of his presidency: the firestorm ignited by the revelation of his extramarital affair with White House intern Monica Lewinsky.

Despite intense public and media pressure about the affair, Clinton continued to fulfill his presidential obligations, among them hosting a state visit by the Prime Minister of the United Kingdom, Tony Blair. On the afternoon of February 6, 1998, after the two heads of state made their customary prepared statements to the press, Clinton Opened the Floor to questions from the reporters. At that point, he became fair game for the subject that was uppermost in the minds of the media and the public. One question came from Wolf Blitzer, the senior CNN political correspondent:

Mr. President, Monica Lewinsky's life has been changed forever, her family's life has been changed forever. I wonder how you feel about that and what, if anything, you'd like to say to Monica Lewinsky at this minute?

The stinging question brought a few scattered titters from the other reporters. Looking straight ahead, right at Blitzer, Clinton smiled and bit his lower lip, an expression that had become his trademark, then said:

That's good!

The crowded room erupted in laughter. After it subsided, Clinton continued:

That's good...but at this minute, I am going to stick with my position and not comment. [7.7]

Blitzer had nailed the acknowledged charismatic master of communication skills at his own game, and the master acknowledged it publicly for all to hear. Fortunately for Clinton, he was able to default to his legal situation and not answer. He provided a valid reason.

Speculative. If you get a question that requires a forward-looking statement, such as, "When will you be profitable?" Don't forecast. In this day and age, after all the financial scandals, leave the predictions to gypsy fortune tellers. Attribute your reason not to provide an answer to company policy.

Guilty as charged. You could be asked a question concerning an issue about which you or your company are guilty as charged. For instance, if your start-up company is entering a sector dominated by a larger company, and you get the question from the previous chapter, "There are dozens of little start-ups doing exactly what you're doing! Then there all those big guys, with their entrenched market share. It's a jungle out there, and you're only just getting off the ground! What on earth makes you think that you can survive?"

Or if you were George H. W. Bush, and Marisa Hall asked, "How has the national debt personally affected each of your lives? And if it hasn't, how can you honestly find a cure for the economic problems of the common people if you have no experience in what's ailing them?"

In each case, the underlying issue is that the question is uncomfortable but true. Start-ups *do* have a difficult challenge, and millionaires such as George H. W. Bush do *not* have personal experience in what is ailing people caught in an economic downturn.

However, neither you nor the president of the United States has to plead guilty to the charge and surrender.

■■■ Guilty as Charged Questions

Here is what George H. W. Bush actually said in response to Marisa Hall's question:

> *Are you suggesting that if somebody has means that the national debt doesn't affect them? [7.8]*

Any answer after that kind of negative statement would be defensive. Here is what he might have done instead:

- **Buffer**. "How can I help you?"
- **Agree**. "You're absolutely right," then, using more of her words, "The national debt hasn't affected me...." The agreement expresses transparency.
- **"But...."** Don't agree too long. Step on the brakes and say, "But...." (There is a proverbial story about the 1,000-word sentence in which the 998th word is *but*, which invalidates all the previous 997 words.) The *but* either diminishes or counterbalances the admission of guilt. After the "But..." pivot, make a sharp U-turn. "...that doesn't mean that I don't care. Everybody cares..." which is where he began his answer— without the Buffer and without the agreement.
- **Evidence**. "As a matter of fact, young woman, I care so much that during my first administration, I initiated an X, and a Y, and a Z program to help people who are less fortunate than I am."
- **Call to action and offer the benefit**. "So if you'll only elect me to a second term, I'll initiate even more such programs."

Just think: If George H. W. Bush had followed this sequence, the world might never have heard of Monica Lewinsky.

Imagine if a start-up company's CEO challenged about "the jungle out there" were to follow the same sequence.

- **Buffer**. "How will we compete?"
- **Agree**. "You're absolutely right; it is a jungle out there." The agreement expresses transparency.
- **"But...."** Don't agree too long. Step on the brakes with a loud "But...." After the "But..." pivot, make a sharp U-turn. "...that doesn't mean that there isn't room for a new entrant."
- **Evidence**. "Those large companies are top heavy and have multiple interests, while our agility and sole focus have netted us 15 major customers in our first year of operation."
- **Call to action and offer the benefit**. "We're confident that we can not only compete effectively, but also will succeed in this market."

In this powerful sequence, the presenter transmits a dynamic wave that has multiple benefits:

- Identifies the Roman Column
- Strips out the negativity
- Acknowledges the questioner's concerns with transparency
- Dispels the questioner's concerns
- Addresses the questioner's concerns
- Concludes confidently

That confident conclusion comes from the last step, which is the presenter's call to action and the benefit to the audience. These terms also can be stated as *Point B* and *WIIFY*.

▪▪▪ Point B and WIIFY

I introduced these terms in my first book, *Presenting to Win: The Art of Telling Your Story.*

- **Point B**: The audience in *any* communication situation begins at Point A, *un*informed, *un*convinced, and *not* ready to act. It is the presenter's objective, goal, or message to move the audience to Point B: informed, convinced, and ready to act. This dynamic shift is the fine art of persuasion. Point B is the call to action.

- **WIIFY**: This acronym (pronounced "whiffy") stands for, "What's in it for you?" based on the more common axiom, "What's in it for me?" The shift from "me" to "you" is deliberate, not just to utilize the power of the "you" word, but to shift the focus from the presenter to the audience. This shift states the benefit to the audience and gives the audience a reason to move from Point A to Point B. People need a reason to act, and it must be their reason, not yours. The WIIFY is the reason.

A simple way to look at Point B is *what* you want your audience to do, and the WIIFY is *why* they should do it.

▪▪▪ Topspin

In Q&A sessions, stating Point B or a WIIFY at the end of the answer to a challenging question produces a strong and confident conclusion. Taken together, this strong ending is called Topspin, from the tennis term for a stroke that hits the ball high, forcing it to bounce sharply, making it difficult for the opponent to return. Topspin in tennis is a power stroke that gives a player a winning advantage. Topspin in Q&A is a power stroke that gives a presenter or speaker a winning advantage. (See Figure 7.1.)

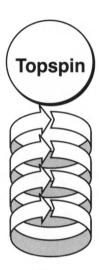

FIGURE 7.1 *Topspin.*

Please note that the icon for Topspin contains multiple upward-swirling arrows; this is meant to encourage you to add multiple variations of your Point B, your call to action, and the WIIFY, the reason for your audience to act. After you have gone through the ordeal of listening, Buffering, and answering tough questions, you have earned the right to promote your own cause and remind your audience of its benefits. Swirl your arrows upward. In your rehearsals, prompt yourself and/or your colleagues by using the gesture that I use when I coach my private clients: Point your forefinger skyward and twirl it: Topspin.

You will learn more about how to add Topspin to your answers in the next chapter, but first an important footnote to the technique of agreeing with guilty-as-charged questions.

■■ Media Sound Bites

Presenters and speakers often deliver their stories to journalists who record the exchange on paper or computer or on digital video or audio files. At that point, the presenter cedes control to the journalist, who is free to reproduce and publish or broadcast any part of the interview out of context.

Therefore, if George H. W. Bush had been in an interview with a reporter instead of in a full length debate and said:

> *You're absolutely right, the national debt has not affected me.*

The reporter could then publish or broadcast those words isolated from the rest of the text and follow it with a commentary, "President Bush admits he doesn't understand the impact of the economy."

Or, if a CEO said to a reporter

> *You're absolutely right; it is a jungle out there.*

The reporter could then publish or broadcast those words isolated from the rest of the text and follow it with a commentary, "CEO admits major obstacles to success."

Therefore, whenever you engage in a media exchange, do not agree with guilty-as-charged questions. Instead, immediately counter the charge:

- "I am fully capable of helping people impacted by the economy."
- "I am fully confident that we can succeed in a competitive environment."

Or, if you want to acknowledge the guilty charge, downplay it as a subordinate clause before your counterstatement.

- "Although the national debt hasn't affected me directly, I can still use the power of my office to *help people* impacted by the economy."
- "Although the competitive arena is a jungle, I am fully confident that *we can succeed.*"

Note that each counterstatement is punctuated with Topspin: "help people" is a WIIFY, and "we can succeed," is a Point B. In the next chapter, you will learn more about this powerful technique by seeing it in action in mission-critical situations.

CHAPTER

8

Topspin in Action

(Martial Art: Agility)

Guard against your opponent, wait for his move then immediately switch to the offensive.

Hei-Ho-Kaden-Sho

(Hereditary Manual of the Martial Arts)

By Yagyu Tajimanokami Munenori (1571–1647) [8.1]

Topspin presents further parallels with the martial arts. It moves the combative exchange from the defensive, deflecting the challenger's negative energy, to the offensive, asserting influence over the challenger. However, exerting that influence is not easy; it requires the presenter to overcome opposing natural instincts. Human beings, when faced with danger, either try to protect themselves or escape the conflict: the familiar Fight or Flight reaction.

Most presenters, when faced with challenging questions, respond with either the Fight reaction: a terse defensive or evasive answer; or the Flight reaction: a short effective answer and then a rush to move on to the next question. For presenters to stand their ground and add another sentence or two of Topspin requires an act of extreme will. To Topspin *well* requires a skill of extreme mental dexterity.

Just how difficult this can be is illustrated in the field of politics where candidates must stand toe-to-toe with their opponents in debate, in front of the public in open forums, or exposed to the press in the glare of the media spotlight.

▪▪▪ Missing a Free Kick

Massachusetts Governor Michael Dukakis had his big moment in the media spotlight during the U.S. presidential election of 1988. As the Democratic candidate, Dukakis had twice debated George H. W. Bush, the then-incumbent Vice President, but was still behind in the polls. Eager to have another chance, Dukakis accepted an offer from ABC Television for a joint appearance 13 days before the election on its *Nightline* series. The Bush team declined the offer, and Dukakis, liberated from television's equal time requirements or a rebuttal from his opponent, had the equivalent of what in football is known as a *free kick*.

However, during the live broadcast, when host Ted Koppel asked Dukakis a challenging question about his ability to lead the country, he replied:

> *I guess the thing that concerns me the most is that I['ve] found it very difficult to give people in this country a real sense of who the real Mike Dukakis is, who I am, what I care about. The kind of deep commitment I have to people and to communities and to this country and why I'm running for the presidency. You know, I've—people have said, well, I'm kind of cool, I don't have enough passion, and so on. I think people who know me know just how deeply I feel about this country and about our future and about public service and why I have been in public service for 25 years. But it's very difficult to convey that. [8.2]*

By concluding his answer with "It's very difficult to convey that," Michael Dukakis spiraled downward, ending negatively. Imagine if the governor had heeded the advice of Master Munenori and *immediately switched to the offensive* by saying instead,

> *People have said, well, I'm kind of cool. Don't have enough passion and so on, but people who know me, know just how deeply I feel about this country, and about our future, and about public service. And why I've been in public service for 25 years. And if they knew the kind of deep commitment I have to people in the communities and to this country, they would vote for me for the presidency.*

"Vote for me for the presidency," would have been Michael Dukakis' Topspin, his Point B, in his campaign against George H. W. Bush.

Imagine if George H. W. Bush, in his 1992 debate with Bill Clinton, had concluded his answer to Marisa Hall by saying, "So if you'll only elect me to a second term, I'll initiate even more such programs." This would have been George H. W. Bush's Point B as well as Marisa Hall's WIIFY.

Eight years later, George H. W. Bush's son, George W. Bush, ran for the presidency and learned how to Topspin the hard way.

■■■ The Evolution of George W. Bush

Then Texas Governor George W. Bush met then Vice President Al Gore in three debates, the last of which took place on October 17, 2000, at Washington University in St. Louis and was conducted in the town hall format (the same format as the one in which his father had looked at his wristwatch and lost track of Marisa Hall's question). In this format, ordinary citizens get the opportunity to question the candidates directly. (There would be no follow-on questions for the son; he had learned from his father's mistake.)

One young woman, Lisa Kee, asked:

> *How will your tax proposals affect me as a middle-class, 34-year-old single person with no dependents?*

George W. Bush replied:

> *You're going to get a tax relief in my plan. You're not going to be targeted in or targeted out. Everybody that pays taxes is going to get tax relief. If you take care of an elderly in your home, you're going to get the personal exemption increased.*

"...take care of an elderly in your home?" His answer ignored the fact that the young woman had said that she has no dependents. Then, with hardly a pause for breath, he went on to say:

> *I think also what you need to think about is not the immediate, but what about Medicare?*

"Medicare?" Now his answer ignored the fact that she was 31 years away from eligibility for Medicare:

You get a plan that will include prescription drugs, a plan that will give you options. Now, I hope people understand that Medicare today is important, but it doesn't keep up with the new medicines. If you're a Medicare person, on Medicare, you don't get the new procedures. You're stuck in a time warp in many ways. So it will be a modern Medicare system that trusts you to make a variety of options for you.

His rambling answer continued to move further out on a limb:

You're going to live in a peaceful world. It will be a world of peace because we're going to have a clear sight of foreign policy based upon a strong military and a mission that stands by our friends. A mission that doesn't try to be all things to all people. A judicious use of the military which will help keep the peace.

He rambled farther and farther away from her question about his tax proposals:

You'll live in world, hopefully, that is more educated so it's less likely you'll be harmed in your neighborhood. See, an educated child is one much more likely to be hopeful and optimistic. You'll be in a world in which fits into my philosophy. The harder you work, the more you can keep. It's the American way. Government shouldn't be a heavy hand. It's what the federal government does to you. It should be a helping hand....

Finally, as George W. Bush wound down his answer, he addressed the Roman Column in Lisa Kee's original question: his tax proposals.

[A]nd tax relief and the proposals I just described...

Then he offered a WIIFY to the 34-year old single person with no dependents:

...should be a good helping hand. [8.3]

"...should be a good helping hand." Spent by his ramble, George W. Bush's WIIFY fizzled. He made it worse by speaking the words without any sense of conviction.

In his rush to Topspin with his own messages about Medicare, world peace, education, a strong military, his philosophy, and government policy, George W. Bush raced past Lisa Kee's question about his tax proposals with only a vague reference to them in his opening statement:

> *You're going to get tax relief under my plan. You're not going to be targeted in or targeted out. Everybody who pays taxes is going to get tax relief.*

He was equally vague in his closing statement:

> *And tax relief in the proposals I just described should be a good helping hand.*

With his rambling answer on subjects unrelated to tax proposals sandwiched between his first and last words, he appeared evasive. As a result, by the time he got to the end of his ramble, his Topspin fell flat in both delivery and substance.

Despite this performance, George W. Bush assumed the office for his first term. However, his advisors knew that he needed to appear more presidential in public, so they set about to make improvements. The result of their efforts became visible less than a year into office when he held a press conference at a high school in his home town, Crawford, Texas, on November 15, 2001.

In response to a question about U.S./Soviet relations, President Bush replied:

> *I believe the U.S./Russian relationship is one of the most important relationships that our country can have.*

The Roman Column in the question was the U.S./Soviet *relationship*, and so his answer immediately and directly related to the question, quid pro quo. Then, after his answer, he said

> *And the stronger the relationship is...*

By restating the Key Word, *relationship*, he linked forward to say

> *...the more likely it is the world will be at peace.*

"The more likely it is the world will be at peace," a WIIFY for the world. Topspin. Then, restating the words, *the more likely*, he linked forward again:

> *The more likely it is we'll be able to achieve a common objective, which is defeat the evil ones!*

"Common objective" is a synonym for Point B; Point B is a synonym for Topspin.

> *...that try to terrorize governments such as the United States and Russia. And we must defeat the evil ones...*

"We must defeat the evil ones," a restatement of his Point B and another Topspin. Because he was in a high school, he also gave the kids their very own WIIFY.

> *...in order for you all to grow up in a peaceful and prosperous world. [8.4]*

As President, George W. Bush continued to improve his skills. After seasoning by the sobering events of 9/11, the economic downturn, and the war in Iraq, he decided to run for a second term. On the day he officially filed to be a candidate, May 16, 2003, he held a brief press conference on the lawn at the White House.

In response to a question from a reporter about his prospects for reelection, George W. Bush said:

> *The American people will decide whether or not I deserve a second term.*

His quid pro quo answer related directly to the reporter's question and earned him the right to move on to his own message, his Topspin:

> *In the meantime, I am focusing my attention today on finding...helping people find work.*

"Helping people find work," a WIIFY for the electorate immediately after his answer, Topspin:

> *And that's where I'm going to be for a while. I want this economy to be robust and strong so that our fellow Americans who are looking for a job can find a job.*

Another WIIFY for the electorate, another Topspin:

> *We've also got a lot of work to do on the security front.*

Here was still another Topspin, this time to reinforce his role as a wartime president, his Point B:

> *As John clearly pointed out, we've got an issue...we're dealing with countries from around the world to make sure that they know that the war on terror continues. No one should be complacent in the 21st century, the early stages of the 21st century, so long as al Qaeda moves. I've told the country that we've brought to justice about half of the al Qaeda network...operatives, key operatives. And so the other half still lives. And we'll find them, one at a time. [8.5]*

"We'll find them, one at a time," a restatement of his Point B, punctuated with determination in his voice and his expression.

In sum, George W. Bush delivered two strong Points B and two clear WIIFYs *after* his answer. Although the Points B and the WIIFYs were not *directly* in line with the Roman Column of his candidacy, the fact that he had provided an answer to the question released him to move on to his own messages, his Topspin.

The lesson here is that as a presenter or speaker, you must earn the right to Topspin by first answering the question. Then, and only then, will your Topspin flow directly and appropriately from your answer.

The CEO of a start-up company challenged by a potential investor concerned about the company's ability to compete against a larger, entrenched competitor could first answer by describing the company's competitive strategy and then conclude with Topspin, "We're confident that we can not only compete effectively, but we will also succeed in this market." Topspin to Point B. The Topspin then directly counters the challenge hurled in the question.

A salesperson challenged by a potential customer about the high price of a product could first answer by describing the total cost of ownership and then conclude with Topspin, "In the long run, you'll actually pay less." Topspin to a WIIFY.

A marketing manager challenged by the executive staff for seeking more advertising dollars in a time of cutbacks could first answer by reviewing the results of the previous ad campaign and then conclude with Topspin, "The ads will generate more revenue." Topspin to a WIIFY.

Topspin serves as the positive Yang to counter the negative Yin in the toughest question. If a question accuses you of being too expensive, too cheap, too small, too big, too late, too early, too light, too heavy, too narrow, too broad, too anything, you can counter the charge with your Topspin. Remember, however, that you must first neutralize the negative with your Buffer and then provide a substantial answer directly related to the Roman Column in the question. If you can, provide supporting evidence as well. After that, you are free to Topspin at will.

Let's return now to the high-stakes arena of political debate for additional examples of Topspin as practiced by masters of the game.

▰▰■ Lloyd Bentsen Topspins

In the U.S. presidential election of 1988 in which George H. W. Bush ran against Michael Dukakis, their vice presidential candidates, Dan Quayle, the senator from Indiana, and Lloyd Bentsen, the senator from Texas, also debated. The format for their single encounter was to respond to questions posed by a panel of journalists. When they assembled in the Omaha Civic Auditorium on October 5, 1988, Senator Quayle was struggling with the stigma of his youth and inexperience, and the journalists, true to their nature, went after his weak spot.

First, Judy Woodruff of the Public Broadcasting Service challenged Quayle's maturity. Then, Brit Hume of *ABC News* took up the cudgel, challenging him twice more on the same subject and, when his turn came, so did Tom Brokaw of *NBC News*:

> *Senator Quayle, I don't mean to beat this drum until it has no more sound in it. But to follow up on Brit Hume's question, when you said that it was a hypothetical situation, it is, sir, after all, the reason that we're here tonight, because you are running not just for Vice President—*

The audience in the auditorium, sensing the intensity of the panelists' pursuit of this vital issue, broke into applause. Then, Brokaw continued:

> *...And if you cite the experience that you had in Congress, surely you must have some plan in mind about what you would do if it fell to you to become President of the United States, as it has to so many Vice Presidents just in the last 25 years or so.*

With a touch of exasperation, Quayle replied to Brokaw's challenge:

Let me try to answer the question one more time. I think this is the fourth time that I've had this question.

Brokaw interjected, holding up three fingers:

The third time.

Brokaw was wrong. It was the fourth time, but in his frustration, Quayle accepted the correction:

Three times that I've had this question—and I will try to answer it again for you, as clearly as I can, because the question you are asking is what kind of qualifications does Dan Quayle have to be president...

Brokaw shook his head from side to side. That was not the question he was asking. Quayle saw Brokaw's negative reaction and tried to reframe his question:

...what kind of qualifications do I have...

But Brokaw continued to shake his head. As if to emphasize his dissatisfaction, he also sat back and crossed his arms. An audience's physical reaction to whether the presenter has heard the question or not is completely involuntary for all human beings—even professional journalists like Tom Brokaw.

Suddenly, Quayle realized that the Roman Column was his *plan* and not his *qualifications*. His eyes widened and his voice rose in confidence to state it:

...and what would I do in this kind of a situation.

Quayle finally got it right, and Brokaw nodded in assent. Quayle went on for a minute to outline what he would do, the plan that Brokaw wanted to hear, the quid pro quo. Then Quayle went on to conclude his answer with Topspin to his qualifications:

> *It is not just age; it's accomplishments, it's experience. I have far more experience than many others that sought the office of vice president of this country. I have as much experience in the Congress as Jack Kennedy did when he sought the presidency. I will be prepared to deal with the people in the Bush administration, if that unfortunate event would ever occur.*

During Quayle's answer, the television image cut from a close-up of Quayle to a wide shot that included Lloyd Bentsen, his eyebrows raised in incredulity.

At that point, Judy Woodruff turned the floor over to Lloyd Bentsen for his rebuttal. He *began* his answer with Topspin:

> *Senator, I served with Jack Kennedy, I knew Jack Kennedy, Jack Kennedy was a friend of mine. Senator, you are no Jack Kennedy. [8.6]*

As powerful and as famous was Lloyd Bentsen's Topspin, there was another more powerful and more famous.

■■■ Ronald Reagan Topspins

On October 28, 1984, incumbent President Ronald Reagan met Walter Mondale, the senator from Minnesota at the Municipal Auditorium in Kansas City in a presidential debate with a format similar to the Quayle-Bentsen match: responding to the questions from a panel of journalists. During the debate, Henry Trewhitt, the diplomatic correspondent for the *Baltimore Sun*, asked President Reagan:

> *You already are the oldest President in history. And some of your staff say you were tired after your most recent encounter with Mr. Mondale. I recall yet that President Kennedy had to go for days on end with very little sleep*

during the Cuban missile crisis. Is there any doubt in your mind that you would be able to function in such circumstances?

Ronald Reagan, known as the Great Communicator, and deservedly so, replied promptly with a crisp three-word answer:

Not at all...

Then, he immediately switched to the offensive with an agile Topspin for the ages:

...Mr. Trewhitt, and I want you to know that also I will not make age an issue of this campaign. I am not going to exploit, for political purposes, my opponent's youth and inexperience. [8.7]

Even his opponent, Walter Mondale, knew he was in the presence of a master of the game, and he laughed along with the peals of laughter from the audience.

■■■ Barack Obama Topspins

Then Illinois Senator Barack Obama met Arizona Senator John McCain in three debates, the last of which took place on October 15, 2008, at Hofstra University in Hempstead, New York. In his closing statement, Obama said:

I'm absolutely convinced we can do it. I would ask for your vote, and I promise you that if you give me the extraordinary honor of serving as your president, I will work every single day, tirelessly, on your behalf and on the behalf of the future of our children. [8.8]

Four years later, President Barack Obama met former Massachusetts Governor Mitt Romney in three debates, the last of which took place on October 22, 2012, at Lynn University in Boca Raton, Florida. In his closing statement, Obama said:

> *[I]f I have the privilege of being your president for another four years, I promise you I will always listen to your voices. I will fight for your families and I will work every single day to make sure that America continues to be the greatest nation on earth. [8.9]*

Two closing statements, four years apart, and the message—almost word-for-word—is consistent. In each, Obama made a call to action:

> *2008: ...if you give me the extraordinary honor of serving as your president...*

> *2012: [I]f I have the privilege of being your president for another four years...*

and in each, he offered a WIIFY for the electorate:

> *2008: ...I will work every single day, tirelessly, on your behalf and on the behalf of the future of our children.*

> *2012: ...I will work every single day to make sure that America continues to be the greatest nation on earth.*

Ronald Reagan and Barack Obama are examples of virtuosos at their best. Neither skill comes easily; each of them is counterintuitive to the natural tendency of results-driven presenters to jump directly to answers and then to keep moving on to the next question. Each of these skills requires an effort to learn. That takes *discipline*, the next of the core martial arts skills and the subject of the next chapter.

CHAPTER 9

Preparation

(Martial Art: Preparation)

The most important part begins even before you put your hand on the sword.

Jyoseishi Kendan
By Matsura Seizan (1760–1841) [9.1]

In the martial arts, the discipline required to learn new skills carries virtually the same weight as the skills themselves. Every martial arts treatise sets forth both the underlying philosophy and the rigorous steps required to achieve mastery. The learning progression of karate is marked by the graduated color coding of the uniform belts. Beginners get a white belt; masters get the coveted black belt. It takes years of disciplined preparation and repetition to ascend through all the levels, and only the best practitioners attain the highest level. Learning to answer tough questions is not as daunting as this challenging sport, but if you are about to face a challenging Q&A session, you should keep in mind Thomas Edison's formula for genius: 1% inspiration and 99% perspiration. Prepare yourself thoroughly before you put your hand on the sword.

■■■ The NAFTA Debate Revisited

Preparation played a key role in the debate about NAFTA between Al Gore and Ross Perot on the *Larry King Live* television program that you read about in Chapter 2, "The Critical Dynamics of Q&A." You saw how Perot flared up when Gore challenged his position on lobbying, but that was only one of many such outbursts during the 90-minute broadcast. Each of the outbursts was provoked by a deliberate strategy that the Gore team had developed in their debate preparation. Their efforts were described in an article in *The Atlantic Monthly* by James Fallows:

> *Gore, meanwhile, spent the two weeks before the debate studying Perot's bearing and his character, while relying on his staff to dig up the goods on Perot's past...[they] prepared an omnibus edition of Perot's speeches, statements, and interviews about NAFTA, and also tapes of Perot in action. Gore studied them on his own and then assembled a team at the Naval Observatory—the Vice President's official residence—for a formal mock debate.*

One of the key members of that team was Greg Simon, Gore's domestic policy advisor. Simon told Fallows about the key strategy that emerged from those sessions:

> *"If you're dealing with a hothead, you make him mad...You've got a crazy man, you make him show it...He'll be fine as long as everybody sits there and listens to him, but if you start interrupting him, he'll lose it." [9.2]*

Gore interrupted Perot repeatedly. In fact, Perot complained to Larry King, to Al Gore, and to the television audience about the interruptions *eight* times during the first half of the program. By midway through, Perot was steaming mad and operating on a short fuse. He pressed ahead with his cause by turning to the camera and addressing the television audience with yet another blast against NAFTA in general, and Mexico in particular:

> *All right folks, the Rio Grande River is the most polluted river in the Western Hemisphere...*

Right on cue, Gore interrupted:

> *Wait a minute. Can I respond to this first?*

Larry King tried to intervene:

> *Yeah, let him respond.*

By now, Perot was not going to let Gore respond:

> *The Tijuana River is the most...they've had to close it...*

Larry King asked:

> *But all of this is without NAFTA, right?*

Gore persisted:

> *Yeah, and let me respond to this, if I could, would you...*

Perot ignored Gore and turned to address Larry King:

> *Larry, Larry, this is after years of U.S. companies going to Mexico, living free...*

Larry King tried to clarify:

> *But they could do that without NAFTA.*

Perot spoke past Gore, directly to Larry King:

> *But we can stop that without NAFTA and we can stop that with a good NAFTA.*

Gore, sitting at Perot's side, interrupted:

> *How do you stop that without NAFTA?*

Peeved, Perot swung around to face Gore and replied testily:

> *Just make...just cut that out. Pass a few simple laws on this, make it very, very clear...*

Quite innocently, Gore asked:

> *Pass a few simple laws on Mexico?*

His anger rising again, Perot shook his head and then dropped it like a bull about to charge and said:

> *No.*

Gore persisted, quietly, but firmly:

> *How do you stop it without NAFTA?*

Icily, Perot replied:

> *Give me your whole mind.*

"Give me your whole mind." Perot addressed the Vice President of the United States as if he was an errant employee! The Vice President of the United States smiled back broadly, and said:

> *Yeah, I'm listening. I haven't heard the answer, but go ahead.*

Chiding back, Perot snapped:

That's because you haven't quit talking.

Gore replied:

Well, I'm listening…

And then for the third time, Gore calmly repeated his question:

How do you stop it without NAFTA?

Perot would not be calmed:

OK, are you going to listen? Work on it! [9.3]

"Work on it!" More disdain and more petulance from Perot. The sum total of all his contentious behavior came a cropper the next day in the public opinion polls: The undecided respondents dramatically swung in favor of NAFTA (please refer to Figure 2.1) and two months later, Congress ratified NAFTA.

Preparation paid off for Al Gore and NAFTA.

▰▰■ Murder Boards

Every nominee for the Supreme Court has to face a confirmation hearing by the Senate Judiciary Committee. These events often become intense encounters because the party out of power wants to do everything it can to make the sitting president—and that president's choices—look bad.

In preparation for the hearing, nominees spend long hours in mock practice sessions called "Murder Boards," which include everything from re-creating the setting in the senate chamber to anticipating the worst-case questions from the senators.

The Murder Boards for Elena Kagan, President Obama's second nominee for the Supreme Court, were described in a post on realclearpolitics.com by political writer Julie Hirschfeld Davis as follows:

> *For several grueling hours each day, Supreme Court nominee Elena Kagan sits at a witness table, facing a phalanx of questioners grilling her about constitutional law, her views of legal issues and what qualifies her to be a justice. They are not polite...Kagan hashes out answers to every conceivable question and practices staying calm and poised during hours of pressure and hot television lights.*

One item in the same article that deserves particular attention comes from Rachel Brand, an attorney who helped President George W. Bush's nominees, John G. Roberts and Samuel Alito, prepare for their confirmation hearings. Ms. Brand said that the purpose of the Murder Boards "'is to ask those hard questions in the nastiest conceivable way, over and over and over....'" [9.4]

Rachel Brand's triple iteration of *over* is the operative point. You'll recall that Verbalization is the process of rehearsing your presentation aloud as you would to an actual audience. That same practice is just as—if not more—important in handling tough questions. Although it may seem sufficient to list the anticipated challenging questions and to craft an answer for each of them, that is not enough. It is far more effective to have someone fire those questions at you and to speak your answers aloud. And you must do it over and over and over. The dynamics of the repeated interchanges in practice will make your responses in real time crisp and assertive.

The Murder Boards approach worked for Justices Kagan, Roberts, and Alito, and they can work for you. In preparation for your next Q&A session, have a member or members of your team fire tough questions at you and Verbalize your answers to them over and over and over.

Think of it as volleying to perfect your tennis game.

■■■ Presidential Elections

Preparation played a key role in the 1960 U.S. presidential election when the underdog challenger, John F. Kennedy, upset the favorite, sitting Vice President Richard M. Nixon, in that famous first-ever televised debate.

The stark differences in how Kennedy and Nixon prepared for that event were chronicled by Professor Alan Schroeder of the School of Journalism at Northeastern University in his book, *Presidential Debates*, in which he wrote:

> *Although both Republicans and Democrats in 1960 compiled massive briefing books—JFK's people called theirs the "Nixopedia"—only Kennedy bothered to practice for the debate with his advisers...[his] predebate preps consisted of informal drills with aides reading questions off index cards....*
>
> *According to Nixon campaign manager Bob Finch, "We kept pushing for [Nixon] to have some give-and-take with either somebody from the staff...anything. He hadn't done anything except to tell me he knew how to debate. He totally refused to prepare." [9.5]*

Kennedy and Nixon also differed in how they prepared to approach the new medium.

The television director of the debate, Don Hewitt (who went on to become the driving force behind CBS' *60 Minutes*), described some of the behind-the-scenes preparation factors in his autobiography *Tell Me a Story*. Kennedy arrived in Chicago three days before the debate to rehearse and even took some time in the late September sun to burnish the tan he had developed campaigning during the summer. Nixon, who was fighting a viral infection, continued to campaign vigorously right up to the day of debate. He arrived at the WBBM-TV studio in Chicago exhausted and underweight, his clothing hanging loosely over his thin frame.

When Kennedy got to the studio, he accepted a light coat of professional makeup. Nixon's aides hurriedly applied a slapdash coat of a product called "Lazy Shave" to his characteristically heavy beard. Professional makeup is porous, "Lazy Shave" is not. Under the hot lights of the television studio, Nixon perspired, making him appear nervous. [9.6]

The Kennedy team had surveyed the studio in advance and advised him to wear a dark suit to contrast with the light gray backdrop on the set, a staple in those days of black-and-white television. Nixon wore a light gray suit that translated into the same monochrome value as the background and made him appear washed out (see Figure 9.1).

There was only one clock in the WBBM-TV studio, which was on the wall over Nixon's left shoulder. Therefore, whenever Nixon spoke, Kennedy could see his opponent and the clock without having to shift his eyes. Alternatively, whenever Kennedy spoke, Nixon had to dart his eyes away from his opponent to track the time.

This being the first televised debate, the candidates were not fully aware of the inner workings of the medium. To create visual variety, television directors alternate images of the person speaking and the person *not* speaking in what is known as "cut-aways" or "reaction shots." As a result, when Hewitt showed reaction shots of Kennedy while Nixon was speaking, Kennedy's eyes barely moved, making him appear alert and focused; when Hewitt showed reaction shots of Nixon while Kennedy was speaking, Nixon's eyes darted, making him appear nervous and shifty-eyed. Ten years earlier, in a campaign for the senate seat in California, Nixon was labeled "Tricky Dicky" by his opponent. In his first solo run for national office, his furtive eye movements reinforced the label.

In one final touch, during Kennedy's closing statement, Hewitt inserted another reaction shot of Nixon who nodded in seeming agreement with his opponent!

© Bettmann/CORBIS

▲ **FIGURE 9.1**   *John F. Kennedy and Richard M. Nixon debate.*

Nixon had held a slim lead in the public opinion polls right up to the day of the debate. The day after the debate, Sindlinger and Company, a Philadelphia research organization, conducted a telephone poll. Those poll respondents who had watched the event on television thought Kennedy had won, and those who had listened on the radio thought Nixon had won. [9.7]

John F. Kennedy took the lead in the polls and held it until his victory in November.

From that moment on, media consultants became as important as positioning strategists in political campaigns and, from that moment on, preparation became an absolute imperative for debates. Although there were no other presidential debates until 1976, they became set pieces every four years thereafter. In each of those years, each candidate, accompanied by key staff members, ramped up for each debate with the thoroughness of the Allies planning for D-Day.

The teams and the candidates review research, brainstorm, and refine their positions, screen their opponent's videos, and hold mock debates with carefully chosen stand-ins. Some even have rehearsal studios built to replicate those of the actual venue.

Over the years, each debate provided lessons for subsequent debates. Cumulatively, the candidates and their campaign staffs have compiled long lists of what to do and, more importantly, what not to do. After more than half a century, the accumulated intelligence about televised political debates has become a sophisticated science. Professor Schroeder's book provides a full chapter with details about how the candidates prepared for their debates:

- 1976: Gerald Ford versus Jimmy Carter
- 1980: Ronald Reagan versus Jimmy Carter and John Anderson
- 1984: Ronald Reagan versus Walter Mondale
- 1988: George H. W. Bush versus Michael Dukakis
- 1992: George H. W. Bush versus Bill Clinton and Ross Perot
- 1996: Bill Clinton versus Bob Dole
- 2000: Al Gore versus George W. Bush

The first edition of this book had a detailed analyis of the 2004 debates. For this edition, let's briefly review that matchup and then move forward to more recent presidential debates.

■■■ 2004: George W. Bush versus John Kerry

In anticipation of the Bush-Kerry debates, their election teams negotiated for months to establish a set of intricate guidelines. They finally came to terms in a Memorandum of Understanding that ran 32 pages and covered everything from the sublime, the rules of engagement, to the ridiculous, their notepaper, pens, and pencils. Every aspect of the debates was covered in excruciating detail, right down to the exact positions and heights of the podiums.

The lessons of history reverberated behind every stipulation: control of the studio temperature to avoid a repeat of the perspiration that betrayed Richard Nixon; control of the town hall audience microphones to avoid a follow-on question like the one that Marisa Hall asked George H. W. Bush; a set of timing signals installed on each lectern to eliminate the darting eyes that dogged Richard Nixon.

▪ ▪ 2008: Barack Obama versus John McCain

In an echo of the 1960 presidential election, the 2008 candidates differed markedly in their preparations for their debates: Barack Obama was as diligent as John F. Kennedy and John McCain was as dilatory as Richard Nixon.

Having leapt from obscurity to global fame with a dramatic speech at the Democratic National Convention in support of John Kerry's candidacy in 2004, Obama deployed his rhetorical skills for his own candidacy in 2008. He spoke on the stump with the passion of his experience as a community organizer, and he prepared for his debates with the thoroughness of his experience as a lecturer on constitutional law. As CNN described it:

> *Barack Obama is reportedly going to Florida for "debate camp"—traditional preparation that includes a sparring partner playing the role of his Republican opponent.*

Having spoken on the floor of the U.S. Senate since 1987, and having campaigned as a candidate for the Republican presidential nomination in 2000 (until George W. Bush defeated him), McCain decided to prepare for his debates, as CNN reported, "on the fly":

> *He spent several hours Sunday at his campaign headquarters working with aides, and he spent several hours in a Pennsylvania hotel Monday afternoon doing the same.*

> *He will follow this "squeeze it in" prep schedule Tuesday as he campaigns in Ohio, and Wednesday around meetings with world leaders in New York.*
>
> *Not until Thursday afternoon and Friday in Mississippi are McCain aides planning to hunker down and devote all the candidate's time to debate prep. [9.8]*

■■■ 2012: Barack Obama versus Mitt Romney

By the time Barack Obama ran for re-election, he had polished his oratorical skills to a fine sheen at the most prestigious lecterns in the world. Throughout his first term, friends and foes alike agreed that Barack Obama is a commanding speaker. Those same friends and foes expected him to easily outshine former Massachusetts Governor Mitt Romney, whose public persona was most often described as "stiff."

But in their first debate on October 3 at the University of Denver, Obama threw the media and the political world into a state of shock with a thoroughly lackluster performance. Obama was so out of character, the usually supportive *New York Times* made its lead story on the morning after the debate, "Romney Wins Debate Praise as Obama Is Faulted as Flat." [9.9]

The immediate reaction to the debate was a torrent of criticism directed at President Obama, with Republicans, as well as many Democrats, accusing Obama of delivering an uninspired and defensive performance. The *Times* story went on to report that Andrew Sullivan, a blogger and strong supporter of the President, tweeted that "this is a rolling calamity for Obama." Sullivan added: "He's boring, abstract, and less human-seeming than Romney!" [9.10]

And Bill Maher, the liberal comedian who had donated $1 million to a "superPAC" backing Obama, joked: "[I] can't believe [I]'m saying this, but Obama looks like he DOES need a teleprompter." [9.11]

Even Obama had to agree. In an interview with radio host Tom Joyner, the President said, "I think it's fair to say I was just too polite because, you know, it's hard to sometimes just keep on saying and what you're saying isn't true. It gets repetitive." [9.12]

In search of an explanation for Obama's tepid showing, veteran political writer Roger Simon wondered, "Perhaps it was mere fatigue that night in Denver. Or overconfidence. Or lack of preparation. Or the altitude." [9.13]

Most likely, it was lack of preparation. We can't be certain just how much time and effort any candidate devotes to preparation, but we do know that on the day before that first debate, Obama made a campaign stop at Hoover Dam and, according to the *Wall Street Journal*:

> ...*complained Monday during a phone call with a campaign volunteer that his aides are "keeping me indoors all the time...making me do my homework." However, a brown tarp blocking the view of the resort's basketball court suggests Mr. Obama has been shooting some baskets between sessions. [9.14]*

In sharp contrast, in the run up to the second debate, set to take place at Hofstra University in Hempstead, New York on October 16, the *Wall Street Journal* reported that Obama had spent

> ...*three days of prep sessions that began Saturday at a five-star resort in Williamsburg...Outside the sessions, Mr. Obama has spent time walking the grounds of the resort, which is set along the James River, and working out at the gym. [9.15]*

Prep sessions are, by nature, highly confidential, but it's safe to say that one of the topics Obama boned up on was the terrorist attack on the U.S. consulate in Benghazi, Libya on the anniversary of 9/11. In the month leading up to the October debate, each candidate's campaign team and their many supporters hurled charges and countercharges of responsibility and irresponsibility at the other. So it was incumbent upon each candidate to have a well-supported argument and to be fully prepared to deliver it under the pressure of a live television debate.

Sure enough, about halfway through the debate, Romney challenged Obama on his handling of the Benghazi attack:

> *There were many days that passed before we knew whether this was a spontaneous demonstration, or actually whether it was a terrorist attack.*
>
> *And there was no demonstration involved. It was a terrorist attack and it took a long time for that to be told to the American people. Whether there was some misleading, or instead whether we just didn't know what happened, you have to ask yourself why didn't we know...*

The President replied:

> *The day after the attack, governor, I stood in the Rose Garden and I told the American people in the world that we are going to find out exactly what happened. That this was an act of terror and I also said that we're going to hunt down those who committed this crime.*
>
> *And then a few days later, I was there greeting the caskets coming into Andrews Air Force Base and grieving with the families.*
>
> *And the suggestion that anybody in my team, whether the Secretary of State, our U.N. Ambassador, anybody on my team would play politics or mislead when we've lost four of our own, governor, is offensive. That's not what we do. That's not what I do as president, that's not what I do as Commander in Chief.*

The forceful statement was followed by a rapid exchange among the debate moderator, CNN's Candy Crowley, Romney, and Obama:

CROWLEY: Governor, if you want to...

ROMNEY: Yes, I—I...

CROWLEY: ...quickly to this please.

ROMNEY: I—I think interesting the president just said something which—which is that on the day after the attack he went into the Rose Garden and said that this was an act of terror.

OBAMA: That's what I said.

ROMNEY: You said in the Rose Garden the day after the attack, it was an act of terror. It was not a spontaneous demonstration, is that what you're saying?

The governor glowered at the president. Obama stared back.

OBAMA: Please proceed governor.

ROMNEY: I want to make sure we get that for the record because it took the president 14 days before he called the attack in Benghazi an act of terror.

OBAMA: Get the transcript.

CROWLEY: It—it—it—he did in fact, sir. So let me—let me call it an act of terror...

OBAMA: Can you say that a little louder, Candy?

CROWLEY: He—he did call it an act of terror. [9.16]

The CEO of a public company whose revenue has not met expectations must be prepared to provide a detailed response to investors in a quarterly earnings call; the CSO of a pharmaceutical company whose drug has failed clinical trials must be prepared to give an explanation to the Board of Directors; the product manager whose product has missed a shipping date must be prepared to offer an alternative plan for a customer. And so must political candidates be prepared to have a response ready for the worst-case scenario when they meet their opponents.

Obama was ready; Romney was not. In his drive to prove that the President was "misleading," Romney missed an important fact; Obama, in his drive to prepare for the issue, knew that fact cold.

Preparation counts.

As you'll see in the next chapter, that pivotal moment, along with Obama's closing statement in the second debate, were to become the turning point in the campaign.

▀▀■ Lessons Learned

Prepare. Anticipate the worst-case scenario. Make a list of the questions you do *not* want to hear. Find the Roman Columns in the tough questions as well as the non-challenging ones. Develop your positions on every major issue, especially the negative ones. Gather your supporting evidence. Do your research. Do all of this well in advance of your mission-critical Q&A session!

Verbalize. Speak your words aloud in practice just as you will during your actual Q&A session. Verbalization is the equivalent of spring training in baseball, previews of Broadway shows, Murder Boards for senate confirmation hearings, and most pertinent, the mock rehearsals that precede political debates. The latter examples have even more specificity and urgency for you. Politicians speak far more often than do ordinary citizens, and even more so during their campaigns. By the time they get down the homestretch to the debates, they have spoken their messages countless times.

You do not have that advantage. Organize practice sessions to prepare for your actual Q&A sessions. Enlist your colleagues to fire tough questions at you. Verbalize your Buffers. Verbalize your answers until they are succinct and to the point. Verbalize your Topspin to every answer. Verbalize repeatedly, like a tennis volley.

This is a technique I recommend to all my private clients, and particularly to companies preparing their IPO road shows, the most mission-critical of all business presentations. I urge CEOs and CFOs to volley their responses to their list of tough questions over and over until their returns of serves snap like whips. I urge you to treat every Q&A session as your IPO road show. Snap your whip.

The importance of thorough preparation was first put forth in 55 BC by the great Roman orator, Cicero:

> *Unless the orator calls in the aid of memory to retain the matter and the words with which thought and study have furnished him, all his other merits, however brilliant, we know will lose their effect. [9.17]*

10

The Art of War

(Martial Art: Self-Control)

*Those who win every battle are not really skillful...
those who render others' armies helpless without fighting
are the best of all.*

General Sun Tzu
The Art of War [10.1]

The martial arts are called "arts" and not "sciences" because success or failure depends more on artful application than on any formula or equation. The central application of these arts is to the battle itself. It is with good reason that General Sun Tzu's 2,500 year-old book is found on the shelves of many modern businesses today. Here in the twenty-first century, its ideas have become a treatise for combat in business, if not a primer for *any* conflict in life. But the good General did not originate the idea of winning without fighting. The concept goes all the way back to the Old Testament, *"He that is slow to anger is better than the mighty"* (Proverbs 16:32).

Fighting is synonymous with the contentious and defensive behavior you saw exhibited by Ross Perot, Alberto Gonzales, John McCain, and Anthony Weiner. Each of them demonstrated negative behavior that produced negative perceptions in their audiences, and none of them won his battle.

Contentiousness is the most damaging of these behaviors because it represents loss of control, the opposite of the desired objective of *Effective Management*. To achieve this positive perception, you must *never* react to tough questions with anger; instead *always* respond with firm, but calm resolve—which brings us full circle back to the Introduction where we set out with a one-word summary of all the techniques in this book: *control.*

▬▬■ The Art of Agility

Agility requires artistry to succeed. Too strong a touch can overshoot the mark; too light can fall short. Martial art masters, athletes, and dancers, all of whom quest for physical agility, understand this all too well. They experience performances of sheer perfection and others of abject failure. The same is true of verbal agility in the line of fire of tough questions.

Al Gore is a case study in point. He won his battle with Ross Perot without fighting when his interruptions caused Perot to lose control and become belligerent. Gore then rendered his opponent helpless by smiling, using agility to counter force.

But Gore forgot his own strategy when he ran for president in 2000. Heading into the presidential debates with George W. Bush, Gore, with eight years as vice president under his belt, had an apparent edge. The issue of *The Atlantic Monthly* that contained the James Fallows article mentioned in the previous chapter had on its cover a caricature of Gore baring feral fangs.

In their first debate, at the University of Massachusetts in Boston, Massachusetts, on October 3, 2000, Al Gore forsook the agility that had served him so well and came out roaring like a lion. Fueled by his disciplined preparation (and very likely, a strong dose of overconfidence), Gore applied all his rhetorical strengths and accumulated knowledge against his opponent. His statements and rebuttals were filled with aggressive and divisive words like "wrong," "not," "differences," "mistake," and "opposite." [10.2]

Public and professional criticism rained down on Gore, implicating not only his haughty attitude, but the accuracy of his statements.

In response, Gore made a sharp about-face and came out like a lamb in the second debate held on October 11, 2000, at Wake Forest University in Winston-Salem, North Carolina. During the 90-minute event, Gore expressed agreement with Bush *seven* times on major issues, undershooting his intended mark by a country mile.

Humbly, at the end of the broadcast, Gore even offered an apology for his exaggerations in the earlier debate.

I got some of the details wrong last week in some of the examples that I used, Jim, and I'm sorry about that. [10.3]

In the third debate on October 17, 2000, at Washington University in St. Louis, Missouri, Gore reversed field again. Swinging back to his aggressive ways, he went on the attack. Keep in mind that this is the very same town hall debate in which George W. Bush, in an answer to Lisa Kee, rambled off track and fizzled. His rambling answer was accompanied by wandering around the open space of the in-the-round setting. In the following section, which occurred earlier in that debate, you'll see Gore's most pronounced attack and, more important, how Bush handled it.

The moderator, Jim Lehrer of the *PBS News Hour* asked Gore:

> *[W]ould you agree that you two agree on a national patient's bill of rights?*

A revved-up Al Gore replied emphatically, "Absolutely not," and then went on to discuss a proposal pending in Congress called the Dingle-Norwood bill, which would provide legislation on health maintenance organizations (HMOs). Gore then went on to say:

> *And I specifically would like to know whether Governor Bush will support the Dingle-Norwood bill, which is the main one pending.*

Lehrer said:

> *Governor Bush, you may answer that if you'd like. But also I'd like to know how you see the differences between the two of you, and we need to move on.*

Bush rose from his seat and began to address his answer to the town hall audience:

> *Well, the difference is...that I can get it done. That I can get something positive done on behalf of the people. That's what the question in this campaign is about....*

As Bush continued, Gore stood up and started to walk across the open space, directly toward his opponent, almost menacingly. Unaware of Gore's move, Bush continued:

...It's not only what's your philosophy and what's your position on issues, but can you get things done?

In the middle of his statement, Bush turned to see Gore approaching.

Bush paused for a beat, then nodded at Gore and smiled, evoking titters from the audience. Then Bush turned back to the audience and said:

And I believe I can.

The audience titters gave way to laughter. Gore stopped in front of Bush and forced a broad smile that stood in sharp contrast to his rigid body language and insisted:

What about the Dingle-Norwood bill?

Lehrer interceded:

All right—yes.

Bush said:

I'm not quite through. Let me finish. I talked about the principles and the issues that I think are important in a patient's bill of rights. It's kind of [a] Washington, D.C. focus. Well, it's in this committee or it's got this sponsor. If I'm the president, we're going to have emergency room care, we're going to have gag orders, we're going to have direct access to OB/GYN. People will be able to take their HMO insurance company to court. That's what I've done in Texas and that's the kind of leadership style I'll bring to Washington. [10.4]

George W. Bush did to Al Gore what Al Gore had done to Ross Perot: He countered hostility with agility and neutralized his opponent. To add insult to Gore's injury, Bush, with a virtual free pass from the moderator, concluded his exchange with strong Topspin; an advantage he neglected to take later in that same debate in his exchange with Lisa Kee.

A poll by the *Wall Street Journal/NBC News* about the effects of the debate on public opinion gave George W. Bush a seven-point advantage over Al Gore.

How did this upset occur? How was the underdog able to give the favorite a run for his money? The answer lies in a dynamic that often occurs in a contest of mismatched opponents: *lower expectations.* All the underdog has to do is show up and not foul up. All George W. Bush had to do was avoid mistakes; anything less than a total thrashing by Gore would be a success for Bush. In fact, the Bush team, intentionally or not, presaged its debate strategy by naming its 2000 campaign jet airplane, "Great Expectations."

The debates were Al Gore's to lose and, given his previous successes and his own great expectations, he did. Of course, George W. Bush did become the president in an election so tight the Supreme Court had to decide the disputed vote in the swing state of Florida, but imagine if Al Gore had dominated the debates as he was expected to?

In the first debate, Gore abandoned agility and became the assailant. In the second, he over-compensated in the opposite direction into passivity. By the third, in trying to reassert his power, he overshot his mark, lost his touch—and lost control.

■■■ The Critical Impact of Debates

George W. Bush also succeeded in duplicating a feat that only his father, George H. W. Bush had accomplished: winning the election despite losing the debates. In the entire history of presidential campaigns, all the candidates (except the Bushes) who succeeded in their televised debates won their elections:

- **1960:** John F. Kennedy defeated Richard Nixon in the election after he bested him in the seminal debate that set the pattern for all other debates to follow.

- **1976:** Jimmy Carter defeated President Gerald Ford after the incumbent self-destructed in the second of their three debates during the Cold War when he said, "There is no Soviet domination of Eastern Europe and there never will be under a Ford administration."

- **1980:** Ronald Reagan defeated Jimmy Carter after their single debate when he notably responded to Carter's position on Medicare by remarking, "There you go again!" Then, even more notably when, in his closing statement, Reagan looked into the camera and asked the nation, "Are you better off than you were four years ago?" one of the most subtle, yet powerful, and often-copied political Topspins.

- **1984:** Ronald Reagan defeated Walter Mondale in a landslide after essentially breaking even in their two debates, but skewering Mondale in the second debate with his memorable Topspin, "I will not make age an issue of this campaign. I am not going to exploit, for political purposes, my opponent's youth and inexperience."

- **1988:** George H. W. Bush defeated Michael Dukakis in the election after losing to him in their two debates.

- **1992:** Bill Clinton defeated George H. W. Bush and Ross Perot with his famous charisma and George H. W. Bush's infamous wristwatch blunder in the second of their three debates.

- **1996:** Bill Clinton defeated Bob Dole with uncontested charisma not only in their two debates, but throughout the campaign.

- **2000:** George W. Bush defeated Al Gore after their three debates in which he surpassed lower expectations while Gore overshot and undershot his higher expectations.

- **2004:** Echoing his father's accomplishment 16 years earlier, George W. Bush defeated John F. Kerry in the election despite losing in all three of their debates. [10.5]

- **2008:** The cool Barack Obama defeated the cantankerous John McCain with a rhetorical advantage described by the *Wall Street Journal*:

  A review of the highlights of Mr. Obama's 2008 debates against Sen. John McCain shows that the famous description of the president's personal style—that he is no-drama Obama—precisely fits the candidate who comes through on a debate stage. [10.6]

- **2012:** No-drama Obama defeated Mitt Romney, a man described in the same article—in the usually supportive *Wall Street Journal*—as "the one who needs drama." And Obama did it with two deft strokes of agility in the second of their three debates. [10.7]

His first was during the exchange with Romney about the attack in Benghazi, which you read about in the previous chapter. Let's revisit the dialogue of that exchange, this time adding the demeanor of each of the candidates as they spoke. In sharp reversal to their first encounter, Obama took charge, while Romney lost his cool.

This debate took place in the town hall format, in-the-round, surrounded by citizens seated on platforms, with the moderator, CNN's Candy Crowley, sitting at the head of the round. Romney and Obama sat on stools in the open space, where they were free to move about to address the audience.

The exchange about Benghazi began when Romney accused Obama of misleading the public:

  It was a terrorist attack and it took a long time for that to be told to the American people. Whether there was some misleading, or instead whether we just didn't know what happened, you have to ask yourself why didn't we know...

An indignant Obama stood and stared angrily at Romney:

...the suggestion that anybody in my team, whether the Secretary of State, our U.N. Ambassador, anybody on my team would play politics or mislead when we've lost four of our own, governor, is offensive. That's not what we do. That's not what I do as president, that's not what I do as Commander in Chief.

As Obama headed back to his stool, Crowley, turned to Romney and said:

Governor, if you want to...

Romney rose from his stool and walked toward Crowley, turning his back to Obama, and said:

I—I think interesting the president just said something which—which is that on the day after the attack he went into the Rose Garden and said that this was an act of terror.

Remaining seated, Obama replied quietly:

That's what I said.

Romney turned sharply to face Obama:

You said in the Rose Garden the day after the attack, it was an act of terror.

Now Romney paused, glowered at Obama, and nodded silently as if to say, "Right?" Then he added testily:

It was not a spontaneous demonstration, is that what you're saying?

Obama stared back and replied calmly:

Please proceed governor.

Romney turned his back to Obama again and headed toward Crowley:

I want to make sure we get that for the record because it took the president 14 days before he called the attack in Benghazi an act of terror.

Still seated, Obama turned to Crowley and said sternly:

Get the transcript.

Crowley held a stack of paper sheets out to Romney, saying:

It—it—it—he did in fact, sir. So let me—let me call it an act of terror...

Still seated, Obama said:

Can you say that a little louder, Candy?

Crowley said it a little louder:

He—he did call it an act of terror. [10.8]

Following the Old Testament's advice, Obama was slow to anger.

For his second stroke of agility in that same debate, Obama followed another piece of advice, this one from Revolutionary War General Israel Putnam, by not firing until he "saw the whites" of his opponents' eyes.

Almost a month before that second debate, *Mother Jones* magazine published a transcript of a surreptitious video taken of Mitt Romney speaking at a fundraiser in Florida during which he said:

There are 47 percent of the people who will vote for the president no matter what. All right, there are 47 percent who are with him, who are dependent upon government, who believe that they are victims, who believe that government has a responsibility to care for them, who believe that they are entitled to health care, to food, to housing, to you name it. That that's an entitlement. And the government should give it to them. And they will vote for this president no matter what. [10.9]

Up to that point, the race had been neck-and-neck in the public opinion polls. On September 4, the RealClearPolitics average showed the two candidates tied in a dead heat at 46.8 each. (See Figure 10.1.)

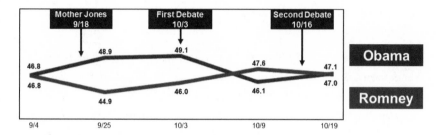

▲ **FIGURE 10.1** *RealClearPolitics averages reflecting impact of the presidential debates.*

But the *Mother Jones* publication of the inflammatory quote on September 18 spread like wildfire. The video clip was played and replayed endlessly on the cable and network news programs, the text was posted all over the Web, and plastered all over the newspapers and magazines. Within one week, on September 25, Romney plummeted to a four-point disadvantage with 44.9 to Obama's 48.9.

Obama carried a lead of 49.1 to 46 into the first debate on October 3 where he had a golden opportunity to bring up the damaging 47 percent quote. But in that uncharacteristically flat performance, he never even mentioned it.

Obama's poor showing in that first debate flip-flopped the poll numbers. By October 9, Romney surged into the lead with a 47.6 advantage over Obama's 46.1.

In that second debate on October 16, Obama roared back into form. He stood toe-to-toe with Romney, vigorously matching him point for point, and even outflanked him on the disputed point about the attack on the U.S. consulate in Benghazi, Libya.

But Obama did not mention Romney's 47 percent quote until *after* Romney's closing statement, when Romney had no chance to respond. Moderator Candy Crowley gave the floor to Obama for his closing statement.

> *CROWLEY: Mr. President, last two minutes belong to you.*

> *OBAMA: ...I believe Governor Romney is a good man. Loves his family, cares about his faith. But I also believe that when he said behind closed doors that 47 percent of the country considered themselves victims who refuse personal responsibility, think about who he was talking about.*

To drive his point home, Obama appealed to the 47 percent.

> *Folks on Social Security who've worked all their lives. Veterans who've sacrificed for this country. Students who are out there trying to hopefully advance their own dreams, but also this country's dreams. Soldiers who are overseas fighting for us right now. People who are working hard every day, paying payroll tax, gas taxes, but don't make enough income.*

Building to a crescendo, he rolled into a Topspin and then to a WIIFY:

> *And I want to fight for them. That's what I've been doing for the last four years. Because if they succeed, I believe the country succeeds.*

Then he became personal:

> *When my grandfather fought in World War II and he came back and he got a G.I. Bill and that allowed him to go to college, that wasn't a handout. That was something that advanced the entire country. And I want to make sure that the next generation has those same opportunities.*

Finally, he capped his closing statement with Topspin to his Point B:

That's why I'm asking for your vote and that's why I'm asking for another four years.

Moderator Candy Crowley Retook the Floor and Romney could not rebut:

President Obama, Governor Romney, thank you for being here tonight. On that note we have come to an end of this town hall debate. [10.10]

Three days later, on October 19, Obama was back in the lead with a 47.1 to 47 lead, an advantage he carried into victory in November. [10.11]

After the election, Public Opinion Strategies, a market research firm that specializes in corporate and public policy research, analyzed the exit polls and found that "Romney lost 18%–81% among voters who said 'cares about people like me.'" [10.12]

▬▬■ Lessons Learned

The mission-critical, white-hot dynamics of presidential campaigns play out on the wide screen of public attention, offering lessons for other candidates—and anyone else who stands up in the line of fire—from which to learn. Unfortunately, some candidates do not take heed of those lessons and, as you will see in the next chapter, pay a painful price.

11

Lessons *Not* Learned

Those who do not learn from history are doomed to repeat it.

George Santayana (1863–1952) [11.1]

■■■ Reaction Shots

You'll recall how, in the landmark 1960 presidential debate between Richard Nixon and John F. Kennedy, reaction shots of Nixon and his darting eyes made him appear nervous and fretful—not presidential—and that the lessons learned from that debate set into place a virtual instruction manual that candidates have aggregated and followed ever since—until 2000, when Al Gore debated George W. Bush.

You'll also recall from the previous chapter how contentious Gore was in his first debate with Bush, using aggressive words like *wrong, not, differences, mistake,* and *opposite.* He compounded that negativity by expressing those combative words in a combative manner, repeatedly punctuating his delivery with condescending sighs, derisive head-shaking, scornful frowns, and disdainful eye-rolls.

The arrogant behavior immediately boomeranged. Television broadcasters had a camera isolated on Gore for reaction shots. Their news directors took the output of this camera, edited his disdainful expressions into a rapid-cut sequence and ran it in their local and national broadcasts.

In the next public opinion poll, Bush, who had trailed by 1.8 points before the debate, moved ahead of Gore by 1.5 points, a net change of 3.3 points. [11.2]

Four years later, the same George W. Bush, eager to take a lesson from Al Gore's failure to learn from history, carefully negotiated a predebate agreement with his Democratic opponent, John Kerry, which stipulated that the television directors could not use isolated reaction shots. The broadcasters—including Fox News, the openly pro-Bush cable channel that provided the pool cameras for all the networks—got around the prohibition by using split-screen shots. For most of the debate, all the channels showed both candidates, so that while one was speaking, the other's reactions were clearly visible.

These split-screen shots boomeranged on George W. Bush. In an eerie echo of Al Gore's behavior four years earlier, it was now the incumbent who repeatedly expressed displeasure as his challenger was speaking. This time, it was with disdainful scowls, impatient frowns, and angry grimaces.

In an equally eerie echo, the television cameras captured Bush's scorn, but this time, it was the Democratic party that leapt to the fore: Within 24 hours after the debate, it posted a page on its website called "Faces of Frustration," which linked to a 43-second video sequence of 14 rapidly cut shots of George W. Bush's peevish looks.

The Bush Scowl and the Gore Sigh were then joined in 2012 by the Obama Grimace. You'll recall how, in that nearly disastrous first debate with Mitt Romney, Obama gave a lackluster performance, manifested by his cast-down eyes and dour expressions evident in the split-screen shots of the CNN broadcast. But Obama added insult to injury by showing disdain for his opponent.

During one of Romney's turns, as he spoke animatedly, Obama's eyes remained cast down.

> *ROMNEY: Dodd-Frank was passed. And it includes within it a number of provisions that I think has some unintended consequences that are harmful to the economy. One is it designates a number of banks as too big to fail, and they're effectively guaranteed by the federal government.*

Obama's eyes, still down, shook his head.

> *ROMNEY: This is the biggest kiss that's been given to—to New York banks I've ever seen.*

As Obama continued shaking his head, he pursed his lips in a grimace and then mouthed, "No."

Undeterred, Romney barreled on to drive his point home.

> *ROMNEY: This is an enormous boon for them. There've been 122 community and small banks have closed since Dodd-Frank.*

At a later point in the debate, during another of Romney's turns, the CNN image again showed both candidates in a split screen. As Romney spoke, Obama's eyes were cast down again.

> *ROMNEY: [T]he key task we have in health care is to get the cost down so it's more affordable for families.*

Obama glanced up to glare at Romney and then back down again.

> *ROMNEY: And then he has as a model for doing that a board of people at the government, an unelected board, appointed board...*

His eyes still down, Obama grimaced.

> *ROMNEY: ...who are going to decide what kind of treatment you ought to have.*

From his side of the screen, Obama, his head down again, said, "No it isn't."

> *ROMNEY: In my opinion, the government is not effective in—*

Obama looked up, turned his head to Romney's side of the screen, and grimaced again. And again, Romney barreled on to drive his point home.

> *ROMNEY: ...in bringing down the cost of almost anything. [11.3]*

▪▪▪ Agreement

For one more lesson *not* learned, let's go back to the Kennedy-Nixon debate. Remember that during Kennedy's closing statement, a reaction shot of Nixon showed him nodding in seeming agreement with his opponent. But that nod was nothing compared to what Nixon said in his *opening statement*:

> *The things that Senator Kennedy has said many of us can agree with. There is no question but that we cannot discuss our internal affairs in the United States without recognizing that they have a tremendous bearing on our international position. There is no question but that this nation cannot stand still; because we are in a deadly competition, a competition not only with the men in the Kremlin, but the men in Peking. We're ahead in this competition, as Senator Kennedy, I think, has implied. But when you're in a race, the only way to stay ahead is to move ahead. And I subscribe completely to the spirit that Senator Kennedy has expressed tonight, the spirit that the United States should move ahead. [11.4]*

In 2000, Al Gore, in apparent reaction to his slippage in the polls after his first debate with George W. Bush, ignored Nixon's lesson and agreed with his opponent *seven* times during their second debate.

In 2012, Barack Obama compounded the errors of his flat first debate by going from one end of the spectrum—disdain—all the way to the other, by showing agreement with his opponent.

During one of Romney's turns, the split screen showed both candidates.

> *ROMNEY: My view is that we ought to provide tax relief to people in the middle class. But I'm not going to reduce the share of taxes paid by high-income people.*

Obama nodded in agreement, contradicting his consistent campaign pledge to raise taxes on high-income people.

ROMNEY: High-income people are doing just fine in this economy. They'll do fine whether you're president or I am.

Obama forced a smile.

ROMNEY: The people who are having the hard time right now are middle-income Americans. Under the president's policies, middle-income Americans have been buried. They're just being crushed.

Obama nodded again, in seeming agreement that his own policies were crushing middle-income Americans.

Later in the debate, Romney stayed on the attack:

ROMNEY: In order to bring the cost of health care down, we don't need to have a board of 15 people telling us what kinds of treatments we should have. We instead need to put insurance plans, providers, hospitals, doctors on target...

Obama began nodding again.

ROMNEY: ...such that they have an incentive, as you say, performance pay, for doing an excellent job, for keeping costs down, and that's happening. Innermountain Healthcare does it superbly well...

Obama continued nodding and said, "They do."

ROMNEY: ...Mayo Clinic is doing it superbly well, Cleveland Clinic, others.

Once again, Romney drove home his campaign position.

ROMNEY: But the right answer is not to have the federal government take over health care and start mandating to the providers across America, telling a patient and a doctor what kind of treatment they can have. [11.5]

Mitt Romney's victorious performance in that first debate, however, was short-lived. In the second debate, as you read in the previous chapter, Obama's revived energy and his checkmate on the sharp exchange about the Benghazi attack put him back in the lead in the polls. (See Figure 10.1.)

By the time the two candidates met for their third debate on October 22, in Boca Raton, Florida, Romney, was in search of a debate strategy that would restore his momentum.

Unfortunately, the strategy he chose ignored Nixon's history lesson: Romney agreed with Obama, and he did so almost twice the number of times Al Gore had agreed with George W. Bush.

Here, from the transcript of that debate, are Romney's Disastrous Dozen Agreements:

1. *...we're going to have to recognize that we have to do as the president has done. I congratulate him on—on taking out Osama bin Laden and going after the leadership in al-Qaeda.*

2. *There was an effort on the part of the president to have a status of forces agreement, and I concurred in that, and said that we should have some number of troops that stayed on. That was something I concurred with...That [was] your posture. That was my posture as well.*

3. After Obama, speaking of his handling of Syria, said:

   What we've done is organize the international community, saying Assad has to go.

   Romney said:

   Recognize—I believe that Assad must go.

4. Obama, speaking of his handling of Libya, said:

   [W]e did so in a careful, thoughtful way, making certain that we knew who we were dealing with, that those forces of

moderation on the ground were ones that we could work with, and we have to take the same kind of steady, thoughtful leadership when it comes to Syria. That's exactly what we're doing.

In his response, Romney said:

I don't want to have our military involved in Syria. I don't think there is a necessity to put our military in Syria at this stage. I don't anticipate that in the future.

5. When CBS moderator Bob Schieffer asked Obama:

[D]uring the Egyptian turmoil, there came a point when you said it was time for President Mubarak to go.

Obama said:

Right.

When Schieffer turned to Romney for his position, he replied:

I believe, as the president indicated, and said at the time that I supported his—his action there...once it exploded, I felt the same as the president did....

6. After Obama said of Romney:

He's praised George Bush as a good economic steward and Dick Cheney as somebody who's—who shows great wisdom and judgment.

Romney said:

My plan to get the industry on its feet when it was in real trouble was not to start writing checks. It was President Bush that wrote the first checks. I disagree with that.

7. After Obama said:

[W]hat I now want to do is to hire more teachers, especially in math and science, because we know that we've fallen behind when it comes to math and science.

Romney said:

Look, I love to—I love teachers, and I'm happy to have states and communities that want to hire teachers do that.

8. *I want to underscore the same point the president [made,]*
   which is that if I'm President of the United States, when I'm
   President of the United States, we will stand with Israel.

9. After Obama said:

   As long as I'm president of the United States Iran will not get
   a nuclear weapon. I made that clear when I came into office.
   …We then organized the strongest coalition and the strongest
   sanctions against Iran in history, and it is crippling their
   economy.

   Romney said:

   And crippling sanctions are something I called for five years
   ago, when I was in Israel, speaking at the Herzliya
   Conference. I laid out seven steps, crippling sanctions were
   number one. And they do work. You're seeing it right now in
   the economy. It's absolutely the right thing to do, to have
   crippling sanctions.

10. When Schieffer asked Romney about the president's plan to
    withdraw troops from Afghanistan in 2014, he replied:

    Well, we're going to be finished by 2014, and when I'm
    president, we'll make sure we bring our troops out by the end
    of 2014.

11. *[W]e look at what's happening in Pakistan, and recognize*
    that what's happening in Pakistan is going to have a major
    impact on the success in Afghanistan. And I say that because
    I know a lot of people that feel like we should just brush our
    hands and walk away. And I don't mean you, Mr. President,
    but some people in the—in our nation feel that Pakistan is
    being nice to us, and that we should walk away from them.

    …This is—this is an important part of the world for us.
    Pakistan is—is technically an ally, and they're not acting
    very much like an ally right now. But we have some work to
    do. And I—I don't blame the administration for the fact that
    the relationship with Pakistan is strained. We—we had to go
    into Pakistan. We had to go in there to get Osama bin Laden.
    That was the right thing to do.

12. When Schieffer asked Romney:

Let me ask you, Governor because we know President Obama's position on this, what is—what is your position on the use of drones?

Romney replied:

Well I believe we should use any and all means necessary to take out people who pose a threat to us and our friends around the world. And it's widely reported that drones are being used in drone strikes, and I support that...entirely, and feel the president was right to up the usage of that technology, and believe that we should continue to use it, to continue to go after the people that represent a threat to this nation and to our friends. [11.6]

After the debate, CNN polled registered voters who had watched the debate and found that 48 percent said Obama won, and 40 percent said Romney did. [11.7]

To culminate this discussion of agreeing with an opponent, let's return to the Kennedy-Nixon debate as a fitting bookend to this chapter—as well as the entire book. Remember that Nixon, in his own opening statement, expressed agreement with Kennedy, and then did it again by nodding during Kennedy's closing statement; which undoubtedly fueled the negative perception of his performance in the debate.

Now let's look at Kennedy's statement and see how he used agreement *effectively*:

If you feel that everything that is being done now is satisfactory, that the relative power and prestige and strength of the United States is increasing in relation to that of the Communists; that we've b[een] gaining more security, that we are achieving everything as a nation that we should achieve, that we are achieving a better life for our citizens and greater strength, then I agree. I think you should vote for Mr. Nixon.

Of course, Kennedy didn't think that any one should vote for Nixon! He was simply making the statement to set up a refutation:

> *...But if you feel that we have to move again in the sixties, that the function of the president is to set before the people the unfinished business of our society as Franklin Roosevelt did in the thirties, the agenda for our people— what we must do as a society to meet our needs in this country and protect our security and help the cause of freedom.*

Having presented his agenda as a better alternative to Nixon's, Kennedy went on to drive home his Point B.

> *...That's the question before the American people, and only you can decide what you want, what you want this country to be, what you want to do with the future. I think we're ready to move. And it is to that great task, if we're successful, that we will address ourselves. [11.8]*

▦▪ Lessons Learned

Of the nearly 313 million citizens in the United States, only two, and on rare occasions, three, of them ever get to debate their fitness for the presidency on live television, and those who do only get to do so every four years. Granted that these examples of presidential shortfalls, although fascinating, are not directly applicable to most citizens, they do reinforce several of the key techniques in this book.

Just as the disdain expressed by Al Gore, George W. Bush, and Barack Obama did not serve them well, it could hurt your cause. To avoid such emotional expressions, you can use Subvocalization and Buffering. Subvocalization, introduced in Chapter 5, "Active Listening," keeps your mind focused on finding the Roman Column rather than reacting to the emotion of the question. Buffering, described in Chapter 6, "Retake the Floor," strips the emotion out of the question.

The agreement with their opponents expressed by Richard Nixon, Al Gore, Barack Obama, and Mitt Romney produced negative effects; only John F. Kennedy skillfully used the technique to his advantage. However, you can use agreement for a positive purpose: transparency. If you are guilty as charged by a tough question, you would do well to agree that it is true and show transparency. In this day and age of rampant evasion by so many public figures, transparency has become almost non-existent.

For example, you may

- Be higher priced
- Be up against a larger competitor
- Be late in delivering as promised
- Have had a down quarter
- Have lost a key customer
- Have had a key executive resign
- Had a delay in your product release
- Have had a product trial that failed

This is not to say that you should capitulate and surrender completely. That would put you into the category known as "Breaking into Jail." (For more on this subject, please see my other Pearson book, *Winning Strategies for Power Presentations*.)

Instead, make your agreement very brief and then say "But," and move on to counter the guilty charge:

- Your pricing is higher because you provide more value.
- You can compete with a larger competitor because you offer a differentiation.
- You have improved and sped up your delivery process.
- You expect a better quarter with new efforts to stimulate new sales.

- You have started a search outreach to find a new executive.
- You have accelerated your production schedule.
- You have made corrections in your product trial.

Then you can move forward to a Point B and/or a WIIFY.

In the next chapter, we'll culminate all the techniques with a positive role model from a most unlikely source, but an expert in the art of war—a military general.

12

The Role Model

During the 43 days of the Gulf War in 1991, General Norman Schwarzkopf, the commander-in-chief of Desert Storm, held only about half a dozen press conferences in the press room in Riyadh, Saudi Arabia. Each of those sessions was very, very brief, but despite such minimal exposure, "Stormin' Norman," as he was known, became an instant global celebrity, garnering huge fees for keynote speeches. He attracted this attention because, in each of those sessions, broadcast live throughout the world, the General exhibited complete command and control in answering the journalists' questions. Schwarzkopf used all the same techniques you've learned in this book and serves a positive role model.

A particular case in point is the press conference of February 24, 1991. After nearly a month of air bombardments, the coalition forces launched a massive ground offensive, and Schwarzkopf appeared to describe the first day's actions to the pool of reporters.

He began the session by reading a brief opening statement that ended with the following words.

> So far, the offensive is progressing with dramatic success. The troops are doing a great job. But I would not be honest with you if I didn't remind you that this is in the very early stages. We are a little more than 12 hours into this offensive, and the war is not over yet.

Then Schwarzkopf removed his eyeglasses and looked out at the sea of reporters and said,

> That concludes my prepared comments and I am now ready to take a very few questions.

"A very few questions." In fact, the entire Q&A session ran just two minutes and 48 seconds in real time, during which he fielded 10 questions. The role model did what you must do in your sessions: *Manage the time.* Schwarzkopf started by setting the audience's expectations, and so must you. When you Open the Floor to questions, you can say that you have no time for questions or that you have all the time in the world, but set the time expectations. Schwarzkopf did, and then proceeded to fulfill them. He continued his time management by counting down the last few questions toward the end.

But let's begin with first things first, when Schwarzkopf Opened the Floor, the first reporter asked:

> *Can you give us an idea of how long, based on what you know now, if things go according to plan, how long do you anticipate this thing is going to last and how do you account for the fact that the opposition has been so light so far?*

A double question, "How long and why so light?" Two related questions. If you get multiple *un*related questions, pick only one, Buffer it, answer it, and then say, "You had another question." Because the reporter's questions were clearly related, Schwarzkopf fielded them both—in reverse order. The "why so light?" was first.

> *First of all I want to say that the opposition has probably been so light so far because of the excellent job that all of the forces have to date done in preparing the battlefield. With regard to your second question, it's impossible to say how long it's going to take...*

"It's impossible to say how long it's going to take," meaning that Schwarzkopf had no intention of answering the other question about forecasting the length of the war. Instead, he said,

> *Let me put it this way. It's going to take as long as it takes for the Iraqis to get out of Kuwait and the United Nations resolutions to be enforced.*

"...the Iraqis to get out of Kuwait and United Nations resolutions to be enforced," was Schwarzkopf's Point B, his Topspin.

If, after your business presentation, you are asked, "How long is it going to take until you release the next version of your product?" you should say, "It's impossible to say how long it's going to take." That's the Buffer using the Roman Column, *time*, as well as the candid answer. When you've done that, you can roll into your Topspin. "...but I can tell you that when the next version is released, it will have the same high quality as all the other products in our powerful pipeline and produce the same rich benefits to our customers." State your Point B and your audience's WIIFY. Seize the opportunity.

General Schwarzkopf then recognized the next reporter, who asked:

> *There have been some reports that there has been an ongoing situation, but can you at least tell us whether we have any forces in Kuwait City? There have been reports of some paratroopers seen over Kuwait City, these reports by Kuwaiti residents.*

The Roman Column in this question was about confidential strategic information the General could not possibly broadcast to a worldwide television audience that was sure to include informants for the opposition. In business, Q&A sessions often occur at conferences where competitors are very likely to be in the audience. No businessperson or soldier has any obligation to reveal strategic information and should never do so. Schwarzkopf asserted his position. He just said, "No."

> *I'm not going to in any way discuss the location of any of the forces involved in the battle to date.*

Without missing a beat, the General then turned to another reporter who asked:

> *General, have any U.S. or allied troops encountered chemical or biological weapons?*

THE ROLE MODEL

"Chemical or biological weapons" are the Key Words in the question. Schwarzkopf rolled those Key Words into his answer as a Buffer.

> *We had some initial reports of chemical weapons, but those reports to date, as far as we're concerned, have been bogus. There have been no reported chemical weapons used thus far.*

Just like Colin Powell, Norman Schwarzkopf used the Key Word technique as his Buffer. And just like Colin Powell, not once during the entire Q&A session did he use a Double Buffer such as, "You'd like to know if our troops encountered any chemical or biological weapons," or a paraphrase such as, "Did our troops encounter any chemical or biological weapons?" In each of the 10 questions he fielded, Schwarzkopf Buffered *only* with the Key Words and rolled them into each of his answers. Remember that the Key Word Buffer allows no thinking time but, when you get it right, the promptness of your response makes you appear sharp and in control.

The next reporter asked:

> *Would you say that things are going better than you expected at this stage or about on par or slightly worse?*

"Better, on par, or slightly worse?" A multiple choice question with three options. Schwarzkopf, being a Topspinner, chose the high ground.

> *So far we are delighted with the progress of the campaign.*

This next question came from a professional reporter who—as someone in your audience is very likely to do—asked a convoluted question, made more so by a halting delivery.

> *With one exception...uh...the...uh...contact with the enemy was described...you say...as light. Can you provide any details at all...*

■ 169 ■

Schwarzkopf started to answer before the reporter even finished.

...about the exception?

Before you see the General's answer, think. Specifically, what does she want to know? Please note that the rest of this page is left blank for you to think about your answer.

The reporter wanted the General to provide details of the heavy engagement. Here is his answer:

> *This afternoon about two hours ago, one of the Marine task forces was counterattacked with enemy armor. The Marines immediately brought their own artillery to bear, they also brought their anti-tank weapons to bear. We also brought our Air Forces to bear and the counterattack was very quickly repulsed and they retreated. I can't tell you the exact number or loss of tanks...*

"I can't tell you the exact number or loss of tanks." In other words, he did not give the reporter any of the details she wanted. His reply was entirely Topspin. "The Marines immediately brought their own artillery to bear; they also brought their anti-tank weapons to bear. We also brought our Air Forces to bear...." In essence, we kicked their butts!

> *...but there were several tanks that were lost in that particular battle.*
>
> *About two more questions.*

"About two more questions." Now he started to count down and, as he did, his answers became shorter and shorter. He also refused to take follow-on questions, which is a privilege you do not have. The next reporter asked:

> *Has the resistance been light simply because the Iraqis are retreating, or are they simply not engaging you, or are they surrendering? What exactly are they doing?*

The epitome of succinctness, Schwarzkopf replied:

> *All of the above.*

Another reporter asked:

> *You say the opposition is light. Is this because you have avoided a frontal confrontation with them, or are you going around, or over, and is that why there is little opposition?*

Schwarzkopf responded:

> *We will go around, over, through, on top, underneath, and any other way to get through.*

The same reporter tried a follow-on question:

> *General, have you gone through sir? Is that why it's light?*

Ignoring him, Schwarzkopf turned to another.

> *One more.*

This journalist asked:

> *General, have you encountered the Republican Guard yet?*

Moving briskly, Schwarzkopf responded:

> *Some.*

This journalist also tried a follow-on question.

> *What kind of resistance have you gotten from that?*

Schwarzkopf also ignored this follow-on and turned to another reporter.

> *Alright last question.*

The last question came from a man with a British accent.

> *General, are you going to pursue the Iraqi soldiers into Iraq, or are you going to stop at the Kuwait/Iraq border?*

Schwarzkopf looked straight at the man and said:

> *I am not going to answer that. We are going to pursue them in any way it takes to get them out of Kuwait.*

Then the General slapped his palm on the lectern, turned on his heel, and walked out, saying over his shoulder:

Thank you very much.

The reporter who had asked the "over and around" question called after him:

General, when will we see you again? Tomorrow at six? [12.1]

The General did not reply. He left his last words trailing in his wake, resonating throughout the press room, and out into millions of television sets around the globe, "We are going to pursue them in any way it takes to get them out of Kuwait," his Point B, his Topspin.

General Schwarzkopf had a number of unique control factors working for him that you and most people in business, and in most walks in life, do not share. In his press conferences, he was the solicited party, and his audiences were the solicitors. In your Q&A sessions, the shoe will be on the other foot: You will be the solicitor, and your audiences, with whom you are trying to do business, will be the solicited. Most of Schwarzkopf's information fell under the cloak of tactical secrecy; most of your business information must be open and above board. Schwarzkopf had no need to give his media audience a single WIIFY; you have an obligation to give your audience as many WIIFYs as you can.

Nevertheless, General Schwarzkopf provides an excellent role model for all the techniques you've learned in this book:

- Manage the time
- Listen intently
- Identify the Roman Column in every question
- Buffer with the Key Word
- Answer succinctly
- Topspin, Topspin, Topspin

▰▰▪ Complete Control

Figure 12.1 is a graphical representation of the dynamics of a conventional Q&A scenario. The first downward triangle in black indicates a challenging question, plunging at you like a dart to the heart. Most presenters, being results-driven, rush to provide an answer, parallel to the question, represented by the downward white triangle. These separate dynamics exert no control and add no value to the exchange.

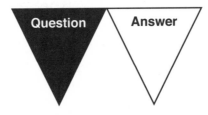

▲ **FIGURE 12.1**   *Conventional Q&A dynamics.*

To assert control in your Q&A exchange, you must listen for the Roman Column during the question with the "empty cup" *concentration* of a Zen master. Then you must intervene with the two upward gray triangles shown in Figure 12.2.

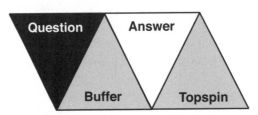

▲ **FIGURE 12.2**   *Controlled Q&A dynamics.*

The first gray triangle is a Buffer composed of a paraphrase or Key Words to level the playing field, the equivalent of self-defense in the martial arts. The second gray triangle, which brackets the answer, is Topspin to your Point B and/or your audience's WIIFY, the equivalent of an *agile switch to the offensive* in the martial arts. These upward thrusts add control dynamics to the exchange. Between the two, you must provide an answer that is the positive Yang to balance the negative Yin in the issue of the challenge.

When most politicians respond to questions, they jump directly to the Topspin, conveniently skipping the answer. In one of the 2000 presidential debates, George W. Bush jumped to his Topspin with an insufficient answer to Lisa Kee's question about his tax proposals. *Skipping the answer appears evasive. Never skip the answer.*

When most businesspeople respond to questions, in their eagerness to provide an effect to a cause, they jump directly to the answer, end the exchange, and then promptly move on to the next question. In the process, they miss the opportunity to Topspin. They offer no Point B and no WIIFY. They make no call to action and give the audience no reason to act. Such behavior exerts zero control.

The winning sequence is

- Question
- Buffer
- Answer with supporting evidence
- Topspin

When you learn all the steps with the discipline of a samurai warrior and apply them with the controlled artistry of a symphony conductor, you combine the up and down dynamics of the triangles in Figure 12.2 and shift their direction—in your favor. You take complete control.

Asserting all these control techniques is no easy matter, for they require an entirely new set of skills that are counterintuitive to the reflexive Fight or Flight behavior triggered when you step into the line of fire. The challenge to achieve control is then doubled:

Overcome the instincts, and learn the new skills. It is a task well worth the effort, for the outcome is also doubled: Survive and thrive without fighting.

P.S. The last sentence in this book is a WIIFY, my Topspin to you. Good luck!

Endnotes

Introduction: Universal Challenges, Universal Solutions

I.1 Theodore H. White, *The Making of the President 1960*, Atheneum House, 1961, page 293.

I.2 RealClearPolitics, General Election: McCain vs. Obama, http://www.realclearpolitics.com/epolls/2008/president/us/general_election_mccain_vs_obama-225.html.

I.3 Alessandra Stanley, "A Question Reprised, but the Words Come None Too Easily for Palin," *New York Times*, September 26, 2008, http://www.nytimes.com/2008/09/26/us/politics/26watch.html?_r=0.

I.4 Past Debates, http://www.2012presidentialelectionnews.com/2012-debate-schedule/2011-2012-primary-debate-schedule/.

I.5 Transcript: Fox News-Google GOP Debate, September 22, 2011, http://2012election.procon.org/sourcefiles/Sep_22_2011_republican_debate.pdf.

I.6 RealClearPolitics, 2012 Republication Presidential Nomination, http://www.realclearpolitics.com/epolls/2012/president/us/republican_presidential_nomination-1452.html.

I.7 CNN Wire Staff, "BP chief to Gulf residents: 'I'm sorry,'" CNN , May 31, 2010, http://edition.cnn.com/2010/US/05/30/gulf.oil.spill/index.html.

Chapter 1: Agility Versus Force

1.1 Press Conference by the President, June 23, 2009, http://www.whitehouse.gov/the_press_office/Press-Conference-by-the-President-6-23-09/.

1.2 Statement by the President on the Sequester, March 1, 2013, http://www.whitehouse.gov/the-press-office/2013/03/01/statement-president-sequester.

Chapter 2: The Critical Dynamics of Q&A

2.1 Dana Milbank, "Maybe Gonzales Won't Recall His Painful Day on the Hill," *Washington Post*, April 20, 2007, http://www.washingtonpost.com/wp-dyn/content/article/2007/04/19/AR2007041902571.html.

2.2 Kashmir Hill, "The Perfect Media Storm That Is 'Weinergate,'" *Forbes*, June 1, 2011, http://www.forbes.com/sites/kashmirhill/2011/06/01/the-perfect-media-storm-that-is-weinergate/.

2.3 "WEINERGATE: Weiner on Maddow 'It could be' my weiner," http://youtu.be/WZ37P7f_5JI.

2.4 NAFTA Debate, Transcript, Courtesy CNN.

2.5 The Second McCain-Obama Presidential Debate, October 7, 2008, http://www.debates.org/index.php?page=october-7-2008-debate-transcrip#.

2.6 Kathleen Parker, "The Town Hall Debate: That One Comment," *Washington Post*, October 8, 2008, http://voices.washingtonpost.com/postpartisan/2008/10/the_town_hall_debate_that_one.html.

2.7 "NY Rep Weiner Goes BALLISTIC on Colleagues for Opposing Healthcare for 9-11 Heroes," http://www.youtube.com/watch?v=3B_I6rgixxY.

2.8 Dana Milbank, "Maybe Gonzales Won't Recall His Painful Day on the Hill," *Washington Post*, April 20, 2007, http://www.washingtonpost.com/wp-dyn/content/article/2007/04/19/AR2007041902571.html.

2.9 Dan Eggen and Michael A. Fletcher, "Embattled Gonzales Resigns," *Washington Post*, August 28, 2007, http://www.washingtonpost.com/wp-dyn/content/article/2007/08/27/AR2007082700372.html.

2.10 David A. Fahrenthold and Paul Kane, "Rep. Anthony Weiner resigns," *Washington Post*, June 16, 2011, http://www.washingtonpost.com/politics/anthony-weiner-to-resign-thursday/2011/06/16/AGrPONXH_story.html.

Chapter 3: Effective Management Implemented

No endnotes

Chapter 4: You're Not Listening!

4.1 The Second Clinton-Bush-Perot Presidential Debate (Second Half of Debate), October 15, 1992, http://www.debates.org/index.php?page=october-15-1992-second-half-debate-transcript.

4.2 The Third Gore-Bush Presidential Debate, October 17, 2000, http://www.debates.org/index.php?page=october-17-2000-debate-transcript.

4.3 The Second Bush-Kerry Presidential Debate, October 8, 2004, http://www.debates.org/index.php?page=october-8-2004-debate-transcript.

4.4 The Second Clinton-Bush-Perot Presidential Debate (Second Half of Debate), October 15, 1992, http://www.debates.org/index.php?page=october-15-1992-second-half-debate-transcript.

4.5 The Second Clinton-Bush-Perot Presidential Debate (Second Half of Debate), October 15, 1992, http://www.debates.org/index.php?page=october-15-1992-second-half-debate-transcript.

4.6 Historical Presidential Zap, April 2, 1992, http://www.actupny.org/campaign96/rafsky-clinton.html.

4.7 The Second Clinton-Bush-Perot Presidential Debate (Second Half of Debate), October 15, 1992, http://www.debates.org/index.php?page=october-15-1992-second-half-debate-transcript.

4.8 *Washington Post*, October 17, 1992.

Chapter 5: Active Listening

5.1 Joe Hyams, *Zen in the Martial Arts*, Tarcher, October 1979.

5.2 The Second Clinton-Bush-Perot Presidential Debate (Second Half of Debate), October 15, 1992, http://www.debates.org/index.php?page=october-15-1992-second-half-debate-transcript.

5.3 The Second Clinton-Bush-Perot Presidential Debate (Second Half of Debate), October 15, 1992, http://www.debates.org/index.php?page=october-15-1992-second-half-debate-transcript.

Chapter 6: Retake the Floor

6.1 Kotoda Yahei Toshida, *Ittosai Sensei Kenpo-Sho* (*Teacher Ittosai Sword Manual*).

6.2 President Obama's 100th-Day Press Briefing, *New York Times*, April 29, 2009, http://www.nytimes.com/2009/04/29/us/politics/29text-obama.html?pagewanted=all.

6.3 Colin Powell Press Conference, April 15, 2003, Transcript, Courtesy CNN.

6.4 Colin Powell interview with Author, March 2013, permission granted.

Chapter 7: Provide the Answer

7.1 Transcript: Republican Primary Debate, October 18, 2011, http://presidentialdebate.org/watch-past-debates/2012-republican-primary-debates-archive/transcript-republican-primary-debate-of-10182011/.

7.2 Republican Debate, February 22, 2012, Courtesy CNN.

7.3 Bush Press Conference, April 13, 2004, Courtesy CNN.

7.4 Bush Press Conference, August 2004, Courtesy CNN.

7.5 The Second Bush-Kerry Presidential Debate, October 8, 2004, http://www.debates.org/index.php?page=october-8-2004-debate-transcript.

7.6 Judson Cox, "Questioning Kerry's loyalty," *RenewAmerica*, March 23, 2004, http://www.renewamerica.com/columns/cox/040323.

7.7 Courtesy CNN.

7.8 The Second Clinton-Bush-Perot Presidential Debate (Second Half of Debate), October 15, 1992, http://www.debates.org/index.php?page=october-15-1992-second-half-debate-transcript.

Chapter 8: Topspin in Action

8.1 Yagyu Tajimanokami Munenori, *Hei-Ho-Kaden-Sho* (*Hereditary Manual of the Martial Arts*).

8.2 *Nightline*, "A Conversation with Michael Dukakis," ABC News, October 25, 1988.

8.3 The Third Gore-Bush Presidential Debate, October 17, 2000, http://www.debates.org/index.php?page=october-17-2000-debate-transcript.

8.4 Bush Press Conference, November 15, 2001, Transcript, Courtesy CNN.

8.5 Bush Press Conference, May 16, 2003, Transcript, Courtesy CNN.

8.6 The Bentsen-Quayle Vice Presidential Debate, October 5, 1988, http://www.debates.org/index.php?page=october-5-1988-debate-transcripts.

8.7 The Second Reagan-Mondale Presidential Debate, October 21, 1984, http://www.debates.org/index.php?page=october-21-1984-debate-transcript.

8.8 The Third McCain-Obama Presidential Debate, October 15, 2008, http://www.debates.org/index.php?page=october-15-2008-debate-transcript.

8.9 President Barack Obama and Former Gov. Mitt Romney, R-Mass., Participate in a Candidates Debate, October 22, 2012, http://www.debates.org/index.php?page=october-22-2012-the-third-obama-romney-presidential-debate.

Chapter 9: Preparation

9.1 Matsura Seizan (1760–1841), *Jyoseishi Kendan.*

9.2 James Fallows, "An Acquired Taste," *The Atlantic Monthly*, July 2000.

9.3 NAFTA Debate, *Larry King Live*, Transcript, Courtesy CNN.

9.4 Julie Hirschfeld Davis, "Kagan practices answers, poise in mock hearings," *RealClearPolitics*, June 23, 2010, http://www.realclearpolitics.com/news/ap/politics/2010/Jun/23/kagan_practices_answers__poise_in_mock_hearings.html.

9.5 Professor Alan Schroeder, *Presidential Debates: Forty Years of High-Risk TV*, Columbia University Press (September 15, 2000), page 80–81.

9.6 Don Hewitt, *Tell Me a Story: Fifty Years and 60 Minutes in Television*, PublicAffairs, October 1, 2002.

9.7 From "Winners of the First 1960 Televised Presidential, Debate Between Kennedy and Nixon," by Sidney Kraus, *Journal of Communication*. Volume: 46. Issue: 4 (1996). Reprinted by permission of Oxford University Press.

9.8 Dana Bash, "Strikingly different debate prep approaches for McCain, Obama: Obama and McCain are starting to prepare for the upcoming debates," CNN Politics, September 23, 2008, http://politicalticker.blogs.cnn.com/2008/09/23/strikingly-different-debate-prep-approaches-for-mccain-obama/.

9.9 Michael D. Shear, "Debate Praise for Romney as Obama Is Faulted as Flat," *New York Times*, October 4, 2012, http://www.nytimes.com/2012/10/05/us/politics/after-debate-a-torrent-of-criticism-for-obama.html?hp.

9.10 Michael D. Shear, "Debate Praise for Romney as Obama Is Faulted as Flat," *New York Times*, October 4, 2012, http://www.nytimes.com/2012/10/05/us/politics/after-debate-a-torrent-of-criticism-for-obama.html?hp.

9.11 https://twitter.com/billmaher/status/253680489850892289.

9.12 Black America Web, "'The Big Chief' Calls Home," *Black America Web*, October 10, 2012, http://blackamericaweb.com/50182/the-big-chief-calls-home/2/.

9.13 Roger Simon, "Presidential debate: Obama snaps back hard," *Politico*, October 17, 2012, http://www.politico.com/news/stories/1012/82509.html?hp=l5.

9.14 Janet Hook, "One Debate Goal: Sway the Swayable," *Wall Street Journal*, October 2, 2012, http://online.wsj.com/article/ SB10000872396390443862604578032742191911924.html?mod= ITP_pageone_2.

9.15 Peter Nicholas and Carol E. Lee, "Town-Hall Format Could Dull Barbs in Second Debate," *Wall Street Journal*, October 15, 2012, http://online.wsj.com/article/ SB10000872396390443624204578056904092211888.html?mod= ITP_pageone_2.

9.16 President Barack Obama and Former Gov. Mitt Romney Participate in a Candidates Debate, October 16, 2012, http://debates.org/index.php?page=october-1-2012-the-second- obama-romney-presidential-debate.

9.17 Moses Hadas ed., *The Basic Works of Cicero*, (The Modern Library, 1951), page 178.

Chapter 10: The Art of War

10.1 General Sun Tzu, *The Art of War*.

10.2 The First Gore-Bush Presidential Debate, October 3, 2000, http://www.debates.org/index.php?page=october-3-2000- transcript.

10.3 The Second Gore-Bush Presidential Debate, October 11, 2000, http://www.debates.org/index.php?page=october-11-2000- debate-transcript.

10.4 The Third Gore-Bush Presidential Debate, October 17, 2000, http://www.debates.org/index.php?page=october-17-2000- debate-transcript. [come back to this]

10.5 Critical Impact of Debates, http:/debates.org.

10.6 Gerald F. Seib, "President's 'No Drama' Style Is a Debate Asset," *Wall Street Journal*, October 1, 2012, http://online.wsj.com/article/SB1000087239639044386260457803033034103030930.html.

10.7 Gerald F. Seib, "President's 'No Drama' Style Is a Debate Asset," *Wall Street Journal*, October 1, 2012, http://online.wsj.com/article/SB1000087239639044386260457803033034103030930.html.

10.8 President Barack Obama and Former Gov. Mitt Romney Participate in a Candidates Debate, October 16, 2012, http://debates.org/index.php?page=october-1-2012-the-second-obama-romney-presidential-debate.

10.9 MoJo News Team, "Full Transcript of the Mitt Romney Secret Video," *Mother Jones*, September 19, 2012, http://www.motherjones.com/politics/2012/09/full-transcript-mitt-romney-secret-video.

10.10 President Barack Obama and Former Gov. Mitt Romney Participate in a Candidates Debate, October 16, 2012, http://debates.org/index.php?page=october-1-2012-the-second-obama-romney-presidential-debate.

10.11 RealClearPolitics, General Election: Romney vs. Obama, http://www.realclearpolitics.com/epolls/2012/president/us/general_election_romney_vs_obama-1171.html.

10.12 Glen Bolger, "The New Electoral Math, and What it Means for Polling," *Public Opinion Strategies*, November 26, 2012, http://pos.org/2012/11/the-new-electoral-math-and-what-it-means-for-polling/.

Chapter 11: Lessons *Not* Learned

11.1 Thinkexist.com, George Santayana quotes, http://thinkexist.com/quotation/those_who_do_not_learn_from_history_are_doomed_to/170710.html.

11.2 Nate Silver, "First Debate Often Helps Challenger in Polls," *New York Times*, October 3, 2012, http://fivethirtyeight.blogs.nytimes.com/2012/10/03/first-debate-often-helps-challenger-in-polls.

11.3 President Barack Obama and Former Gov. Mitt Romney, R-Mass., Presidential Candidate, Participate in a Candidates Debate, October 3, 2012, http://www.debates.org/index.php?page=october-3-2012-debate-transcript.

11.4 The First Kennedy-Nixon Presidential Debate, September 26, 1960, http://www.debates.org/index.php?page=september-26-1960-debate-transcript.

11.5 President Barack Obama and Former Gov. Mitt Romney, R-Mass., Presidential Candidate, Participate in a Candidates Debate, October 3, 2012, http://www.debates.org/index.php?page=october-3-2012-debate-transcript.

11.6 President Barack Obama and Former Gov. Mitt Romney, R-Mass., Participate in a Candidates Debate, October 22, 2012, http://www.debates.org/index.php?page=october-22-2012-the-third-obama-romney-presidential-debate.

11.7 Paul Steinhauser, "CNN Poll: Nearly half of debate watchers say Obama won showdown," CNN Politics, October 22, 2012, http://politicalticker.blogs.cnn.com/2012/10/22/cnn-poll-who-won-the-debate/?hpt=po_t1.

11.8 The First Kennedy-Nixon Presidential Debate, September 26, 1960, http://www.debates.org/index.php?page=september-26-1960-debate-transcript.

Chapter 12: The Role Model

12.1 Schwarzkopf Press Conference, February 24, 1991, Courtesy ABC News.

Acknowledgments

For Power Presentations, Ltd.:

Jim Welch is technically the CPA of my company, but he is much more than that. His invaluable acumen helps me to run the business and frees me to deliver the programs that form the basis for this book. Jim is also a wise counsel in matters human and spiritual. As if all of that were not enough, Jim, who attained the Do rank of 4.0 Kyu in Shotokan Karate, validated the martial arts analogies. In fact, Jim is a Black Belt Master in life.

Nichole Nears and Jennifer Turcotte also helped me operate the company, but their contributions to this book went far beyond the call of duty. Together, they performed as a research engine that out-Googled Google. Nichole also generated all the line art with the precision of an architect, tracked down the permissions with the due diligence of an attorney, managed the manuscript with the authority of a drill sergeant, and still had time to be our Web Master. Jennifer handled the source videotapes with the thoroughness of a producer and pre-screened them with the eye of a director. Surely, Ben Affleck will star her first film. Cousin Joel Goldberg, an image-maker par excellence, lent his images and talents generously.

For the source videos:

Kenn Rabin of Fulcrum Media Services went to the ends of the earth to find and, in some cases, unearth the many video and film clip examples that support my concepts. Kenn did his searching with the patience of a monk and the knowledge of a Talmudic scholar.

Brian Fulford, the Senior Licensing Agent of CNN, provided the bulk of the source videos and was a repository of camera angles himself.

Ed Rudolph and Bob Johns, the editors who helped me grab the still frames for the book, are artists-in-residence at Video Arts, San Francisco, a superb production house managed by Kim Salyer and David Weissman. David is no relative, but I wish he were.

Rich Hall contributed mightily to the evolution of the source videos.

For the book:

Bill Immerman, my attorney, who produced the superb film, *Ray*, during the writing of this book, still found time to provide his astute counsel.

Arthur Klebanoff, a rare agent who understands ink-stained wretches because he is one himself.

Paula Sinnott, the editor of the first edition, found new values in material that took me nearly two decades to develop; Jeanne Glasser Levine, the editor of the second edition, added even more new value.

Katie Matejka and Lori Lyons, the Pearson project editors, guided the manuscript through the complex shoals of the production process with the steady assurance of harbor pilot.

Chuck Elliot plastered many green Post-its throughout an early version of the manuscript, all of which helped me to move it to a more mature version with the blazing speed of a Curt Schilling fastball...much faster than Pedro Martinez ever could.

Quentin Hardy, whose PDA and mind are filled with valuable information from Beowulf to Burlingame and beyond.

Eric Nielsen, Senior Director, Rights and Permissions, The Gallup Organization, always exercised his attention to detail, a most suitable trait for a statistician.

Warren Drabek tracked permissions relentlessly.

For their inspiration:

Mike Wallace, Senior Correspondent for CBS *Sixty Minutes.* Heaven did help me.

Babette Cohen did not blow my cover.

Melvin Van Peebles was a reality check at every step along the way, as always.

The late Kelsey Selander Phipps pointed me to the platform. The late Harry Miles Muheim, American, my first speech teacher and a superb writer, taught me to "Keep going," and became the ultimate mentor for the whole shooting match.

As a teacher on my own, I am always mindful of the Rogers and Hammerstein song from *The King and I*, in which a teacher sings of being taught by her students. Many of my student-clients have challenged me, queried me, tested me, disagreed and agreed with me, but they have all taught me to look at my own material more scrupulously and to make improvements constantly. I am particularly grateful to Vani Kola, the CEO of Certus, a company that helps other companies in the line of fire of the Sarbanes-Oxley Act. Vani's astute perceptions during her Q&A session with me added dimension to both the program and the book.

I am also grateful for the stimulating input from many people at Cisco Systems, among them Sue Bostrom, James Richardson, Peter Alexander, Toby Burton, Kaan Terzioglu, Corinne Marsolier, Mary Gorges, and Joe Ammirato; and from many people at Microsoft Corporation, among them Jeff Raikes, Mike Nash, Kai Fu Lee, Yuval Neeman, Pascal Martin, Vince Mendillo,

Sara Williams, Ilya Bukshteyn, Dave Mendlen, Kristin Buzun, and Paul Sausville.

I am equally grateful to Microsoft alumni: Jon Bromberg, the Max Bialystock of video; Paul Gross straightened the long and winding road from Scotts Valley; Rich Tong, the champion of champions; John Zagula, who recently went through his own initiation into the literary fraternity, still found the time to give me the right sequence, the right title and, as he always does, the metaview; and Jonathan Lazarus, both a CBS and a Microsoft Emeritus and an ongoing trusted advisor, whose most memorable contribution was a Redmond-to-New York-to-Las Vegas parlay that rivaled Tinkers-to-Evers-to-Chance.

In a category all by himself is the man who bridges both the Cisco and Microsoft worlds from his lofty perch as a patron saint, Jim LeValley.

In Show Business, the closing act is reserved for the star of the show. For this Road Show, that position goes to the Impresario who, with the panache of a Sol Hurok, started it all, Benji Rosen.

INDEX

Numbers

47 percent quote (Mitt Romney), 146-149

60 Minutes (television program), 8

A

accusations, responding to, 82

Active Listening

  concentration

    importance of, 43-46

    Roman Columns, 46-51

  subvocalization, 51-52

  understanding the question, 53-54

  visual listening, 52

  YAC (yards after catch), 55

agility, 105-106

  Barack Obama example, 117-118

  force versus, 5-6

  George W. Bush example, 108-114

  Lloyd Bentsen example, 114-116

  Michael Dukakis example, 106-108

  Ronald Reagan example, 116-117

  self-control in, 138-142

agreement

  in televised debates, 155-161

  transparency in, 162-163

Alito, Samuel, 124

answering questions

  about presented content, 69-70

  agreement and transparency in, 162-163

  anticipating challenging questions, 91-93

  buffers

    benefits of, 70-71

    double buffers, 73-76

    key word buffers, 72-73, 79-85

  confidentiality, 96-98

  consequences of not listening, 30-42

  control in, 174-176

  defensively, 58-59

  evasively, 94-96

  false assumptions, 93

  General Norman Schwarzkopf example, 166-173

  guilty as charged questions, 98-104

  irrelevant questions, 67

  management of answers, 91

  multiple questions, 67-68

  negative questions, 66

N

NAFTA (North American Free
Trade Agreement), 11,
16, 120-123
names, calling questioners
by, 25
negative behavior
audience perception of,
16-17
contentiousness, 11-16
defensiveness, 10-11
in IPO road show,
consequences of,
17-18
negative questions, 66
netroadshow.com, 18
Night Beat (television
program), 8
Nixon, Richard M., xvi,
125-128, 143, 152, 155,
160-161
North American Free Trade
Agreement (NAFTA), 11,
16, 120-123

O

Obama, Barack, xvii, 2-4,
14-15, 68, 117-118,
129-132, 134, 144-149,
153-160
Obama/McCain debate, 14-15,
117, 129-130, 144
Obama/Romney debate,
117, 130-134, 144-149,
153-160
oil spill in Gulf of Mexico
(2010), xix
open the floor (Q&A
cycle), 24

P

Pace, Julie, 3-4
Palin, Sarah, xvii
paraphrasing challenging
questions, 59-66, 78
benefits of, 70-71
double buffers, 73-76
key word buffers, 72-73,
79-85
Parker, Kathleen, 15
perception, behavior and,
7, 17
consequences of negative
behavior, 16-17
in IPO road shows, 18-19
Perot, H. Ross, 11-14, 16, 31,
38-39, 50, 58, 120-123,
138-139, 143
Perry, Rick, xvii, xix, 89-90
Point B, 101, 111, 113
political conventions,
"bounce," 36
Powell, Colin, 79-85, 93
practice. *See* preparation;
verbalization
preparation, 119-120
Bush/Kerry debate, 128
for challenging
questions, 22
Gore/Perot debate, 120-123
importance of, 134
Kennedy/Nixon debate,
125-128
murder boards, 123-124
Obama/McCain debate,
129-130
Obama/Romney debate,
130-134
presented content, questions
about, 69-70